Moses said:
I have never been eloquent,
O my Lord, please send someone else.
Exodus 4:10,13

TABLE OF CONTENTS

LIST OF EXERCISES

The following exercises can be done in an airplane seat, on a train or bus, as well as at home:

FOREWORD

Rarely does a teacher have a student as multi-talented as Marianne Bahmann. I had the privilege of being her voice professor at Drake University.

At that time the Drake-Des Moines Symphony held annual auditions for young artists. The winners were awarded solo performances with the orchestra. There were four divisions in the auditions and Marianne won three of them: she sang, she played the piano and she had an orchestral composition performed.

Marianne was inducted into Mortar Board at Drake University and also was awarded a Fulbright Scholarship for voice study in Germany. In addition to being an accomplished singer, superb accompanist, teacher, director and coach she expands her skills by continuing to compose and to write.

Coping with the Limelight includes many references to well-known artists and their experiences in dealing with the inner beast, stage fright. These interestingly written accounts should certainly give encouragement to any performer. It is a rare artist who does not get some form of "performance nerves." How comforting it can be to the reader to be led into this realization.

Our author does not leave us here without answering the question: "But how can I cope?" In addition to her personal knowledge and experience she has done extensive research and brings to the reader a comprehensive, motivating and applicable manual. This includes an extensive listing of resources available on the subject of stage fright. I can heartily recommend it to both the beginner and the professional performer.

I suggest that the reader, after scanning the table of contents and reading the preface, turn to the very last page of the manual and read the closing paragraph; then return to page one.

† Andrew B. White,
Professor Emeritus of Voice,
College-Conservatory of Music,
The University of Cincinnati

PREFACE

Stage fright. Who has never experienced the feeling once termed "the bacillus that strikes the brain" when facing the public?

I played my first solo piano recital at the age of thirteen. That afternoon I was terrified, and I discovered that my racing heartbeat and icy, uncooperative fingers were a price I would pay for sharing my talent in public. At first I thought that being scared meant there was something wrong with me that didn't affect other performers. The ones I talked to admitted they felt a little nervous, nothing more. My intense anxiety was apparently a sign of weakness, a lack of professionalism.

Or was it? During the following years and into adulthood, as I continued performing in spite of my fear, I scoured the shelves of libraries and bookstores (this was before the Internet made searching easy) to find anything that could shed light on what I endured. The more I read, the clearer it became that I was not exceptional at all. Many highly successful people in all areas of public life have suffered, and still suffer, from extreme nerves that handicap their presentation. Yet they persist. Why, I asked myself, don't they quit? Why don't I quit? Why do we put ourselves through the agony? How do others cope?

Many articles, books and seminars on the subject of performance anxiety give helpful advice, but each takes a particular line. Do what I tell you, the author says, and you will be fine. But this certainly wasn't always true, at least for me. And there were so many methods! Life was too short to try all of them.

I kept on performing because in spite what I felt each time I went on stage, the urge to express something within myself was stronger than the extreme nervous anxiety and psychic pain I experienced. I want to encourage others who face the limelight in spite of fear to continue. If you are one of them, you are not alone. And you are not crazy or neurotic! With some targeted knowledge and a modicum of effort, you can lower your fear level and control your symptoms as I did.

Years of research and hundreds of private conversations have convinced me that there is no one-size-fits-all method for combating stage fright. There is no magic bullet. It is through trial and error that we find the most effective personal method for handling what many professionals call "the inner beast" that tries to sabotage our best efforts.

Chapter one examines the nature of this destructive force from various angles. Chapter two describes the different battles ordinary folks face when exposed to the spotlight, and what many have done to win them. Chapter three contains candid personal accounts of how they faced the beast by some of our greatest, most successful performers. Of particular importance to them is an acknowledgement that technical perfection will not banish the fear, and that such an expectation produces not security but despair.

Chapter four describes common snares and setups that can intensify and even provoke anxiety if we are not aware of them beforehand. Chapter five details some of the crutches and anchors we use to control our symptoms and explains the differences between them.

Chapter six gives pointers on how to handle unconscious triggers such as personal shyness or an inability to make small talk that can result in a heightened level of pre-performance nerves. Chapter seven provides a capsule history of performance traditions that have contributed to stage fright for many, and how change is happening to many of those traditions. Chapter eight takes the reader step by step through a typical performance day, up to and including the first moments on stage. Finally, chapter nine encourages everyone who has an anxiety attack when facing the limelight to do a post mortem at home.

Examples of basic relaxation and breathing exercises are included where appropriate; a list of them appears at the front of the book for easy access. The annotated reference list at the end of the book is just a sampling of the wide variety of materials available.

Personal accounts of the great artists of the past can be found in any good performing arts library. I was fortunate to have the use of the music collections in Stanford University's Green Library. My special thanks go to Associate Professor Andrea McCook of the Flagler College theatre department for her helpful insights on actors; to my husband Manfred for his encouragement and editorial help, and to Chris Berlin for his original cover concept. The other illustrations from the Dover Clip Art Series are intentionally eclectic; I want them to convey the universal reach of performance anxiety. Finally, I dedicate this manual to the memory of Professor Andrew Broaddus White, voice teacher par excellence. Professor White, who died shortly after writing the foreword to this manual, trained generations of nervous young singers at the

University of Michigan, Drake University, Baylor University, and the University of Cincinnati College-Conservatory of Music. He approached each one with the same patience, dedication, and persistence that he gave to the struggles he faced in his own distinguished career. Andrew White was one of the great interpreters of Mendelssohn's Elijah, and those who heard him mourn the passing of the rich, powerful baritone voice that moved so many.

CHAPTER ONE:
THE NATURE OF THE BEAST

Symptoms strike without warning.
The college recital hall was hot and stuffy on a September evening in the days before public spaces were climate-controlled. The audience of students, professors, and music-loving townspeople lingered in the airy lobby until the

five-minute warning bell sounded. Then they wandered into the hall, clapped down the sticky wooden seats and slid into them. Fanning themselves with their programs, they waited for the first faculty recital of the season to begin.

Backstage the steamy air crackled with tension. The evening's soloist, Professor Alfred Lange, head of the college piano department and a veteran performer, paced up and down in a state of high anxiety. Only a few trusted students knew the source of their silver-haired professor's panic: after forty years of successful concertizing, he had developed an intense fear of forgetting the music.

The symptoms began several years earlier when he suddenly forgot where he was in an opening number. Startled, he managed to find his way back and finish the piece, but the experience unnerved him. He told himself that if it happened again, he would simply bring the piece to a close and move on to the next one.

But he was unable to shake off the growing feeling of uncertainty. Gradually he became so obsessed with the mere thought of forgetting that his mind began to play tricks on him, and his stumbling increased. After a year of this he decided to turn down any future engagements, pleading a heavy teaching load. But there was one obligation he could not avoid: his college contract required him to play an annual faculty recital. Barring illness, he had to appear or lose his job. It would be seven long years until retirement released him from this nightmare.

It was past eight fifteen. Still the soloist paced frantically up and down in the wings, grabbing one music score after another from the arms of a student assistant, flipping wildly through the pages, checking and rechecking for potential trouble spots. In the steamy auditorium, people shifted in their creaky seats. Where was Professor Lange?

Finally at 8:29 the houselights dimmed and he strode out. Looking neither to the right nor the left and ignoring the polite applause, he positioned himself on the cushioned black piano bench, adjusting its height by turning the knobs on either side. He loosened the sleeves under his tuxedo jacket, flexed his fingers, and staring stonily into the raised lid of the grand piano, plunged into the opening runs of Bach's Chromatic Fantasy and Fugue.

It was an unwise choice for an opening number. Momentum carried the soloist through the broken chords of the fantasy, but trouble hit with the intricacies of the fugue. As the second and third voices entered, the pianist desperately tried to outrun his panic by playing faster and faster, scrambling for notes, until he finally blanked completely and the chaotic playing came to a halt.

The professor got up and wordlessly left the stage. After a few moments the house manager appeared and announced to the stunned audience that the professor was ill and could not complete the program. It would not be rescheduled.

I was one of Professor Lange's piano students, and I was backstage that evening. I saw how fear completely overtook him. The shaky knees and cold hands I suffered on stage were nothing in comparison to the terror I saw in my teacher's eyes that night. I wanted to understand what had happened to him. Would my own nervousness deteriorate into that kind of panic? How did the great performers cope with its sudden onslaught, its blind curves? For years I had devoured any article that appeared on the subject. Now I was determined to find out how to turn a nightmare experience for many into what it should be: the expression of a unique creative power and a wonderful gift to be shared.

The beast within.

Stage fright. Performance anxiety. *Lampenfieber*. Fear of the spotlight. Topophobia. Call it what you will. Many factors trigger the panic even in seasoned veterans. It is no respecter of age, sex, or experience. It hits when you are the center of attention and even when you are not. It can develop gradually or come on suddenly. It may be the first or the twentieth or the fiftieth time you are in the spotlight; even an intense desire to perform cannot protect you from its debilitating effects.

Webster's Third Edition dictionary defines stage fright as "Nervousness or panic felt by a person appearing or due to appear before an audience." The audience may be just one person, perhaps a close friend or family member, and you could be standing in your living room. You don't need a stage or a spotlight to feel your knees turn to rubber, your hands sweat, your voice croak, your mind go blank, your throat tighten ...

In discussing the phenomenon, violin teacher Carl Flesch describes a "stage fright bacillus [which will] always find its culture base in the weakest point of one's technical ability or psychic disposition."[1] What a great image! The beast, or bacillus, acts like a moveable blob that prowls and probes around in your brain, searching for soft spots to bore into—attacking your bow arm, your breath support, your memory and your self-confidence.

Television weatherman Willard Scott developed panic attacks in the middle of a long career and underwent intensive treatment before he could face the camera again. Comedian Buddy Hackett stopped live performing after fifty years when he developed dizziness and a feeling that he couldn't breathe on stage. Baritone Robert Merrill had sung "The Star-Spangled Banner" in public hundreds of times, yet forgot the words before thousands of football fans in Yankee Stadium. Actor Laurence Olivier, singers Barbra Streisand and Carly Simon, to name just a few among many, interrupted successful performing careers because of overwhelming stage fright. Pianist Glenn Gould, a Bach specialist, finally played only under carefully controlled conditions in a recording studio. What you may be feeling yourself has happened to many people.

The following diary entry of a nineteenth-century singer named Marianne Lincoln is unusually candid. In 1844 the soprano, an experienced English recitalist, traveled to Germany to continue vocal studies and establish a concert career in Europe. Always confident and self-assured when she sang in England, she describes the shock she felt at her own reaction on the night of her German debut at the Gewandhaus in Leipzig:

"Oh how can I express the uncomfortable situation I was then in. Shivering with cold & timidity, finding myself the object of attention & notice from everybody. A hundred eyeglasses raised to examine the Debutante, who was trembling at the novelty of her position, anxious of course to shine in the eyes of so critical a Public. I felt almost overcome by nervousness & I think I never felt it to such an extent before. Every effort I used, to check it, only served to increase it, &, although I felt completely angry with myself, I could not rally my spirits.

"I was in a truly pitiable condition, when the Overture was ended, & Mr. Gade gave me his hand, to lead me to the Orchestra. I actually wished I could have fainted – anything to have given me a little more time. Unfortunately, too, it was an air of Handel's, that requires sostenuto, & my breath came so thickly, that I was almost choking. My knees trembled under me. How I got through it, I know not. I did not break down. I only recollect my heartfelt joy, when I arrived at the concluding shake, & that I did tolerably well. The audience applauded me very well and were very indulgent."[2]

Lincoln was obviously shaken by her unexpected physical symptoms. It had not occurred to her that the importance of the German debut could so debilitate her. She was not expecting the racing heart, shortness of breath, and tight throat. And by choosing for her first number a slow, sustained Handel aria, she fell into the same trap that ensnared Professor Lange: tradition demands that you open a recital with Handel, Bach, or Scarlatti, composers who require great physical control and concentration.

❦

Why do we lose control?

All of creation reacts to stress. Flora wilt, fauna take flight, earth shakes. Fox and deer prick their ears at the slightest rustle. You and I sense a potential threat and our bodies too prepare for fight or flight. Yet, as performers we are required to develop a third reaction. Under the stress of the spotlight we must stand and deliver. We have to suppress the inner voice that screams: Run!

Being "on" pulls you in two directions at once. When performing you need total inward concentration to keep your wits sharp and your body under control. But at the same time, an outward pull is coming from the presence of the audience. You try to focus, as their energy draws you to them. Lecturers and standup comedians feed on that "back and forth" energy and try to engage the audience. But many solo musicians need absolute quiet in a darkened auditorium to concentrate. Rustling programs, a cough, the slightest whisper—all can awaken the beast and arouse anxiety.

Ron, a young pianist friend, suffered from clammy hands and sweaty fingers whenever he played in public. Frustrated by never doing his best because his fingers slipped and slid on the keys, he gave up piano solo performing and decided to develop his pleasant tenor voice. After a semester as a voice major he was surprised to find during his first student recital that while now his fingers were sweat-free. a new symptom arose. His hands remained dry, but so did his mouth. A lack of saliva caused his throat to catch whenever he took a breath.

Shifting problems are a nuisance for amateurs and professionals alike. Flawless, symptom-free performances are almost unknown. Dancers fall, singers crack, actors forget their lines, pianists' fingers freeze or sweat. Seasoned performers know that physical things can happen, and they go with the flow even when the burden of a successful career becomes heavier to sustain than amateurs can imagine. The more famous you are, the more expensive the tickets to your event become, and the greater is the need for a knockout performance every time. Talk about pressure!

No magic pill has been invented that can completely free everyone from anxiety when we step into the spotlight. The human race is too diverse. We have different natures, different needs, different vulnerabilities. Our homes and family histories, our nervous systems and genetic makeup—many factors influence how we handle stress.

Some of the most tragic cases are long-time performers who suddenly develop terrible anxiety symptoms. Actor Sir Laurence Olivier describes in his autobiography the horrible night after his pregnant wife Joan lost her baby and panic fear gripped him on the way to the theater. He was scheduled to do a run-through and dress rehearsal of Ibsen's The Master Builder. As he put it, "Now, in the time between the dress rehearsal and our first performance, an appalling thought possessed me: 'I think I'm too tired to remember it.'" He struggled from line to line through gritted teeth, his voice fading and his throat closing up, and somehow made it through the ordeal.

For five and a half years Olivier, one of the twentieth century's greatest actors fought the inner beast that persistently tried to destroy his composure on stage. Finally, after a well-received performance of The Merchant of Venice, Olivier gave

THE NATURE OF THE BEAST

himself permission to retire gracefully from the stage without feeling like a failure.[3]

My young friend Ron, the pianist-turned-singer, was determined to have a performing career and resolved to meet the challenge of nerves head on. Under the guidance of his voice teacher he practiced relaxation techniques that helped control his breathing. He increased the flow of saliva by rubbing the sides of his tongue against the edges of his back teeth. This worked quite well. Then he landed the tenor lead in the college spring musical. On opening night he began to "click into another space" as he described it, singing in a hazy fog that only lifted when the final curtain came down.

Afterwards, Ron checked anxiously with friends: "How did I do? Did I disgrace myself?" They looked at him, puzzled. They hadn't noticed a thing. He had performed well, they all agreed. Ron knew then that he would not fight the trance-like feeling if it happened again. While it was a nuisance, in the end it was a harmless outlet for his nerves. Ron has since gone on to have a successful professional career in musical theatre.

Triggers exist. Anxiety happens. Forgive yourself. Then work as hard as you can to tame your beast!

CHAPTER TWO: FACING YOUR FEARS

Coping with the jitters in everyday life.
Pity the person who has to present a work report first thing in the morning after tossing and turning all night. Or the clergyperson who stands before a congregation week after week, year after year, suffering from intense stage fright each time! Hard to believe, but many face this challenge.

Lutheran pastor and columnist Walter Wangerin, Jr. revealed that he would pray every week throughout his career for God to remove this thorn in his flesh. It never happened, but he didn't give up. He described the Sunday-morning anxiety many pastors endure:

> "I wake at 5, I don't eat because I can't. My internal self is as unstable as water. But when I meet the people, my external self has donned a smile, speaks softly, touches everyone and moves to worship with aplomb. And lo: I preach. And ... I do succeed .... But when Saturday comes again, I pace again, wild-eyed and terrified."[4]

You don't even have to be the one up front to feel such anxiety. At times, people suffer real symptoms when someone they care about is under the gun. Call it exaggerated empathy—the dizziness, palpitations, and nausea are real even if you are just a bystander. A case in point is the woeful father-to-be suffering morning sickness and labor pains!

A friend described an experience she had when her pastor husband preached a trial sermon for a church position they both wanted very much. He was calm and collected in the pulpit while she sat dizzy and nauseated in the pew. After the sermon, all her symptoms disappeared.

People who appear in front of others—musicians, actors, dancers, teachers, pastors, bible study leaders, comedians—do not often talk about their bouts with anxiety. Perhaps they think it will hurt one's reputation to admit what appears to be weakness. If asked, they downplay the intensity of their feelings, as in: "Well, sure, I get a little nervous; doesn't everybody?" But these unresolved panic attacks can lead to a sense of isolation and despair that ultimately results in counterproductive, even physically destructive behavior.

Some musicians I know try to dull the pain by playing mind games. They convince themselves that they don't care how they come across. But they pay a high price for such put-on nonchalance. The result is usually sloppy, inaccurate playing lacking the sparkle and excitement that a little nervous energy brings. Add the swagger of an I-don't-care stage presence, and such performers may as well not go on because they quickly lose contact with their audience.

The same applies to the use of drugs and alcohol before going on. We will discuss this subject in detail in a later chapter. For now, let's just say that handing over control of your faculties to a mind-altering crutch at the very time you most need full possession of them is senseless. You'll never know that you weren't invited back for another gig because you weren't fully there the first time.

Most of us, however, do care—a lot—about what is, after all, a unique personal gift. There may be a hundred lyric-soprano voices in your neck of the woods, yet not one of them sounds exactly like you. Sharing your talent enriches everyone who hears or sees you.

One final important note. Because you care so deeply, be aware that the urge to be perfect can arouse the beast. If you feel that your self-worth is on the line every time you appear, you will tie yourself in knots. Step back; do a reality check. Ask yourself: *From whence cometh my fear of flubbing?. Has someone been messing with my head?* Imprint the following mantra on your mind: *There is no perfection in this life. I find joy in the challenge.*

Run, hide, or stand and deliver?

A perceptive person once observed that half the world's work is done by people who don't feel well. How often we drag through our work days! But we dig in and hope we accomplish something in spite of how we feel.

If you must deliver a lecture while fighting a splitting headache, you are in the company of half the world's lecturers. If your half never showed up, the other half would make all the music, lead all the meetings, dance all the Sugar Plum Fairys. Wouldn't that be a shame?

The same applies to performing under the stress that comes from deep panic. The Internet provides thousands of sources dealing with performance anxiety from every aspect.. Type in a generic search phrase such as stage fright, panic attack, or topophobia, and you will be bombarded with information sources. But where to start?

Choose a particular angle; narrow your search. Add a term like "breathing" or "shaking" to pinpoint your problem. Most titles will strike a chord in someone; none will apply to everyone. Remember: there is no magic one-size-fits-all solution! Avoid sites that promise to solve all symptoms They usually turn out to be blatantly commercial and misleading.

Few people know that British author Agatha Christie dreamt of becoming a concert pianist before she turned to writing mystery novels. In her autobiography, Christie describes how she studied and worked hard for years toward her performing goal. But in the end she could not conquer her intense fear. Her teacher confirmed Christie's own suspicions when she advised the young pianist that she "did not have the temperament to play in public." The author describes her decision to quit as follows:

"If the thing you want beyond anything cannot be, it is much better to recognize it and go forward, instead of dwelling on one's regrets and hopes. Such a rebuff coming early helped me for the future; it taught me that I had not the kind of temperament for exhibition of any kind. I can describe what it seemed like by saying that I could not control my *physical* reaction."[5]

One wonders what this world would have been like without Christie's Hercule Poirot and Miss Marple. If the author had been born fifty years later, with the new insights and information we have available today she might have conquered her fears and become a renowned performer—and never written a line. What a loss that would have been for mystery lovers everywhere!

Another young performer made a different decision. In her biography of British pianist Myra Hess, Marian C. McKenna describes how young Myra faced up to her terrible anxiety and decided to continue pursuing a concert career:

> "Shortly before her next Prom [London Promenade concert series] engagement she set out for a long walk on Hampstead Heath, carrying in her pocket a sharp knife, determined to lacerate her fingers so severely that she would be unable to play the next day, and perhaps forever. Along the way she began to waver in her resolve, wondering where she could find the courage to inflict such a terrible injury on her hands.
>
> "After a long struggle with these conflicting emotions she found herself incapable of using the knife, and put it away. Slowly an awareness dawned that if once she permitted herself to commit such an act, she would constantly be seeking a cowardly escape from life's difficulties, and if allowed to bypass this crisis she might never again find the will to face the ordeal of public performance. Resolutely, she retraced her steps toward home, exhausted emotionally but sensing that blessed relief that comes with the knowledge that a fearful decision has been reached and passed."[6]

The confrontation Myra Hess had with herself reveals how completely traumatizing stage fright can be, even for a highly motivated person. She never conquered her fear. Yet throughout a long and distinguished career she stuck by the decision made in deep despair on that walk through the heath. Many have gone through this fire and emerged with the strength of tempered steel, as we shall see in the following chapter.

CHAPTER THREE: THE COMPANY OF THE GREAT

The wayward bow.
Spanish cellist Pablo Casals had no qualms about admitting his lifelong stage fright. On his first tour of the United States, during a climb on California's Mount Tamalpais a falling rock smashed his right hand. He later recalled his first reaction

on seeing the injured fingers: "Thank God, I shall not play the cello anymore."[7]

Casals began his first Vienna concert in such a state of nerves that when he drew his bow across the string for the first note, the bow shot from his hand and flew into the front rows of the audience. Silently someone handed it back to him, and he began again. He says that this incident broke through his nervousness completely and he played one of his best recitals that night.[8]

Leopold Auer, renowned teacher of many professional violinists, said that a violinist's nerves can be most debilitating when they cause the bow to tremble. Some great violinists suffered this agony every time they played in public. Joseph Joachim, for example, once performed the Beethoven violin concerto in such a state of agitation that he didn't even realize he had finished the first movement. Auer relates that on another occasion, when Auer himself was conducting the orchestra, Joachim's bow trembled badly on a sustained trill. Quickly Auer signaled to the orchestra to move on to the next chord, earning a grateful look from the anguished soloist.[9]

Russian violinist David Oistrakh nearly passed up the prestigious 1937 Brussels competition, which he won, because of anxiety. According to Oistrakh's own letters and the testimony of his son, the violinist often suffered so much that he would become physically ill. Imagine his feelings one night at Carnegie Hall in New York when he walked out onto the stage and saw four great stars of the violin world—Fritz Kreisler, Nathan Milstein, Mischa Elman, and Isaac Stern—smiling up at him from the front row! But that evening he went ahead anyway, and played beautifully.

On another occasion Oistrakh was terrified of the double harmonics at the end of a concerto. Unsure whether he could bring them off, he asked the two first violinists of the orchestra to join him in playing them. Unfortunately, the two agitated orchestra players botched them completely while Oistrakh played them perfectly.[10] Unlike Joseph Joachim, Oistrakh could maintain physical control in spite of his panic.

Argentine pianist Martha Argerich in a documentary film about her fifty-year professional career revealed that she suffered terrible panic. Her knees sometimes trembled so badly that her feet banged the floor. Unlike pianist Myra Hess, she actually cut a finger so she wouldn't have to play a concert and stopped performing altogether for several years.[11]

❦

Singers confess all.

Greek operatic soprano Maria Callas had an iron will and strong determination. But these qualities did not protect her from a paralyzing fear of performance. Callas became particularly afraid on those occasions when she did not feel she was in good voice. Of course this is understandable, and for years she managed to perform in spite of this anxiety. But when she reached star status, added to this fear was the feeling that she carried a terrible responsibility because of fame itself. As she confessed in a late interview, "The more I grew in reputation, the more frightened I got."[12] Once in a while she had to be forcibly pushed on stage by her manager. Toward the end of her career, as her voice and health declined, she became dependent on injections and pills to perform.[13]

American baritone Robert Merrill insists in his autobiography that almost all performers are frightened before they go on. He describes the terrors that artists such as Swedish tenor Jussi Bjoerling and American soprano Rosa Ponselle had to face. Ponselle, relates Merrill, often became so ill from tension that she had to cancel appearances. She withdrew from public performance entirely at the height of her operatic career and became a respected teacher. "I was always so afraid," she told Merrill. "You know, I had to fight myself to come out on that stage. And I always hoped, when I walked around the theater, that I would become sick, or have an accident, so I could cancel."[14]

Italian tenor Luciano Pavarotti described the feeling just before going on as "being paralyzed." Even the extroverted Italian tenor Enrico Caruso made no bones about his extreme nervousness. "Of course I am nervous," he said. "Each time I sing, I feel there is someone waiting to destroy me, and I must fight like a bull to hold my own. The artist who boasts he is never nervous is not an artist—he is a liar or a fool."[15] Soprano Lillian Nordica describes the same thing: "In a moment like that there is no such thing as being natural; to be so would mean to turn and flee."[16] Italian operatic soprano Renata Tebaldi describes an occasion at Milan's La Scala opera house in which an insecure high note in the first act of Verdi's "La Traviata" upset her so much that she lost her composure for the rest of the evening. "I don't remember a single thing of what happened in the following acts," she recounts. "I sang the opera to the end, but I felt as if I were in a coma—I knew nothing of what I was doing. I was like a robot."[17] My young friend Ron, who suffered the same thing each time he sang, could say amen to that.

☦

Ignace and Oscar try to quit.

Polish pianist Ignace Paderewski tells in his memoirs of the panic he felt when his first Paris concert resulted in further engagements. Paderewski had worked up one concert program to such perfection that he felt absolutely secure in all the passages of all the pieces. This was highly important to him. He had analyzed his intense fear and determined that it came from a bad conscience. If something in the program was not absolutely secure in his fingers, he reasoned, he would be afraid during the whole concert. But Paderewski's one secure program was such a success that he was forced to continue performing, which meant playing a larger repertoire.[18] Throughout his career, although he traveled and played all over the world, he always suffered violently and even gave up playing in public entirely for a while.

American pianist Oscar Levant described his anxiety symptoms in clinical terms: "Before the concert all the strength left my body. It was unbearable neurotic hysteria which included a psychogenic paralysis. During the performance I lost my coordination. I managed to finish the concert but after that ordeal I declared a hiatus."[19]

Levant did play again, however. While performing a concerto at the Hollywood Bowl, the previous experience came back to haunt him so vividly that at the end of the first move-ment he got up and said to conductor André Kostelanetz, "I'm going to walk off the stage." Startled, Kostelanetz im-mediately gave the downbeat for the second movement and Levant finished the concerto.[20]

✺

And the beast goes on.

Actress Jane Fonda suffered so much from nerves that she almost stopped acting. "I don't want to be scared anymore," she told an interviewer. She recalled that as a young acting student at Lee Strasburg's studio in New York, she and Marilyn Monroe sat at the back of the room to avoid being called on. It worked.[21] But their fear didn't stop them from going on to face the camera.

The Beatles sometimes threw up before live stadium shows. Actor Richard Burton, tenor Jussi Bjoerling and oth-ers have gotten by on the strength of their talent and their reputations even though they went on stage drunk, putting a heavy burden on colleagues to cover mistakes.

Golfer Charles McGrath describes a duffer's dilemma: "There's no anxiety quite like the first-tee jitters: the sweaty palms, the dry throat, the fluttery stomach. And no humiliation quite as awful as that occasioned by the lousy shot that's almost sure to follow. You want nothing more than to become invisible."[22]

The sports world has finally admitted after decades of denial that many players would benefit from professional help for their nerves. It took them a long time to acknowledge a psychological component to the field of sports medicine. Even today, people in the business still insist that debilitating nerves are just part of the game. If you freeze on the mound or blank out when the ball comes toward you, deal with it. Don't go looking for a shrink.

Outfielder Jim Eisenreich (who was finally diagnosed with Tourtette's disease), star rookie pitcher Rick Ankiel, and New York Mets legend Dwight Gooden are only three of many who endured this prejudice when they sought help for performance problems. The Mets broke the psychological logjam in 1988 when they hired psychiatrist Dr. Allan Lans to work full-time with the players. But the Mets management felt they needed to disguise Dr. Lans's true role until he was fully accepted by the players. "We consider him the head of our employee-assistance program," explained the executive responsible for bringing Dr. Lans on board.[23]

Orchestral woes.

Although orchestra players may not seem exposed—they are, after all, performing as a community—many of them also suffer severe stage fright. Some research indicates that they feel the most pressure of all.

Orchestra members have time between entrances to recuperate their energies. But the mental concentration required to count forty measures of rest accurately and then float a perfect flute solo passage can be excruciating.

A scientific study was done on the occasion of the seventieth anniversary of the Vienna Symphony Orchestra. Researchers monitored the physical and psychological effects of performance on the players. The results showed that, even for those with many years of experience, stress was a significant problem for most of them. In fact, each section of players—winds, strings, brass, percussion—felt it was under more stress than the others. Some players reported that the anxiety about missing important cues "resulted in profuse perspiration and trembling or coma-like conditions."[24]

According to the report, orchestra musicians rarely discuss with their colleagues their common fear of miscounting interlude measures: "This phenomenon is considered to be inevitable and part and parcel of the profession."[25] While this stiff-upper-lip attitude is understandable, and shared as we have seen by some in the sports community, the study found clear evidence of permanent circulatory and cardiac stress in the musicians, a heavy price to pay for stoicism.[26] The 1981 report was an important step forward in taking stage fright out of the shadows and making performance medicine a respectable field of specialization for physicians.

☙❧

Why do it?

Whether you experience dry throat, trembling bow arm, breathlessness, coma-like state, nausea, shaky knees, memory loss—the symptoms vary widely—many continue to come back for more. Why? Why do people put themselves through it?

We do it because we have to. As a child I spent hours alone in the backyard, imagining myself on the glamorous stage of the old Metropolitan Opera House singing along with the glorious voices I heard every Saturday on the radio broadcasts. Not to fulfill that dream was unimaginable. I didn't make it to the Met, but I sang and acted on other stages in spite of a lifelong struggle to contain the beast in my brain. I am grateful for every minute of it. Yes, it takes a special push to face the limelight, to expose yourself for better or worse, to fight the urge to give up. But the inner urge to go out there is even stronger for most of us. We performers need to use our talents. Giving up is not something we want to do, nor do we have to in this age of possibilities.

As you contemplate your future as a performer, speaker, ball player or group leader, take your courage from the ones who have gone before us, leaving behind a rich heritage in spite of their personal struggles. A great host stands watching in the wings of history, urging us on. Buoyed by their example, you too can find the path to success. Do it!

CHAPTER FOUR: SNARES
AND SETUPS

Snares.

1. I didn't expect the panic.

New performers often feel traumatized the first time they actually stand up alone in public. Ensnared by their physical reaction to stress, they vow never to go through that again.

It seems so easy just to quit! But—is it?

I once met an actress whom I had admired in local theatre productions for years. Janet played character parts
in a way that was strikingly real. I told her how much her
performances meant to me and asked if she was currently
working on a play. Her expressive face darkened. "Oh, no,"
she said intensely, "I finally got the poison out of my system."
Surprised by this response, I changed the subject. Afterwards
I regretted my cowardice. Because of my fear of prying, I had
missed a chance to let her share her personal struggle with
a sympathetic listener. She had certainly given me an opening.
I suspected that she, too, had fought the stage-fright beast.
If that was the poison in her system, like many of us she felt
driven to perform because suffering through it was better
than not knowing what might have been.

Not knowing what might have been—can you live with that
knowledge?

You have no idea how you will react the first time you are
in the limelight. To find out, you have to do it. Will you bask in
the glow of you audience's undivided attention? (*Who doesn't?*
you may ask.) Or will you find yourself battling the urge to
turn and flee?

Only if you ride a ski lift will you know how it feels to
dangle in a chair twenty feet above the ground. Only if you
sing a solo, preside over a meeting, or stand in a pulpit will
you know how much being the center of attention can jangle
your nerves. Like becoming pregnant or going on a job interview, performing involves risk. Being in the spotlight is an act
of courage for each of us, every time. But you can learn to
deal with it.

The first time country singer Randy Travis set foot
on the Grand Ole Opry stage, his great goal, he nearly
lost it:

"No stage, anywhere, it don't matter the amount of people in the audience, no stage has made me feel like the Opry, has scared me so bad. By the time I finished my first two songs and came off, I was literally to the point of shaking. Done gone all to pieces!"[27]

Probably not a soul in the audience saw his anguish. And that Opry experience didn't stop Randy Travis. A motivated performer, he went on to have a long, successful career.

The difference between people who suffer performance anxiety and people with phobic fears is that we performers will not go to any lengths to remove the feared object or situation from our lives. We need the audience, the stage, the podium or the pulpit to exercise our talents. We are powerfully motivated to overcome whatever physical manifestations the beast in our brain seeks to produce in us. *And we can win that battle!*

2. My job requires it.
Professor Lange, my college piano instructor, knew that he had to play at least one solo recital a year. When he signed his contract, that obligation didn't matter because he didn't have a problem. But a few years later, as his memory began to play tricks on him, the annual concert came to haunt him.

You can be blindsided by a work situation beyond your control. A former boss of mine—I'll call him Larry—was a good administrator but a shy man, terrified of speaking in public. He could avoid this until a new job description required him to deliver an annual oral report in front of the whole department. The first year he called in sick and someone else read his report. The second year he managed to show up, but when his turn came he stayed seated in a chair, eyes glued to the paper, and mumbled his report in an unintelligible monotone. After several years of this, Larry left for a position without the odious obligation. He had been unable to overcome the inner beast.

Job interviews are a nightmare for many people. The stress can be so bad that they stay in a dead-end job rather than face an interviewer. For these sufferers, however, there are remedies that work very well. Interview classes are offered in many community colleges and adult education forums. Through role playing, question-and-answer sessions, and friendly feedback from people in the same situation, you acquire the knowledge and tools to build confidence and present yourself to the best advantage.

Professional church workers and laypeople often dread being asked to give an impromptu prayer. While they have no problem reading a written-out text, an unexpected request can bring on palpitations. Sally, an experienced Christian education leader, never got over this fear. In an article she expresses well what many feel: "There is no moment of panic greater than that invoked by the words, 'Sally, will you please lead us in prayer?'" Sally was no wimp—she kept her cool when she was padlocked into a Latin American airport by machine-gun-wielding police—but in fear of being taken off guard, she always carried a prewritten, all-purpose prayer with her.[28]

3. I was talked into it.
You may be urged into the spotlight by enthusiastic friends and family. Your singing style may be so unique that they insist everyone must hear you. But you don't like to do it because every time you get in front of the mike you panic. When you explain that performing makes you sweat and shake and is definitely not for you, they dismiss your fears as silly. They

simply refuse to listen, and you don't know how to say no without disappointing the people you love.

Wayne, a high-school trombone player, tried hard to get his extended family off his back. Parents, aunts, uncles, cousins, they were all so proud of him! He was, after all, first trombone in an award-winning high school band. He didn't mind playing the concerts or marching at games, but he hated recital solos. He got so scared that he threw up beforehand. He didn't see why he had to endure that; the world was full of trombone players. Finally he got up the nerve to tell his parents that the upcoming spring recital would be his last one. He played his pieces well, and afterwards as he hung around at the back of the hall, relieved, a stranger came over to him. "Wayne," he said, "I really enjoyed your playing. You have a mellow tone that really got to me." Poor Wayne—he didn't want to hear that. He didn't want to care. But maybe he did have something he should share ...

Performers are not interchangeable like spark plugs. Each of us has a special look, a unique sound, an individual message.

We touch people in different ways. *Never devalue your talent just because you are afraid of the limelight!* Even if you decide you can't take on the beast at the moment, keep your skills honed; don't let them wither away. As you go along life's journey, things change. You may want to try it again. Stay in shape and be ready!

4. I really love my craft, but ...
Perhaps you weren't talked into performing by friends and family, but you made a conscious decision that you want to do it. You embrace its risks and hard work—at least in the abstract. You enjoy the preparation, whether in a practice room, on a field or alone at the computer. The act of singing, dancing, preaching, running energizes you. The excitement of the arena pulls you in. But—how to free yourself from the irritating physical symptoms that threaten to sabotage your performance?

The information in the following chapters will be crucial for you. Of all the things that can "trap" us into performing in spite of our fears, love for our craft is the prime motivator to overcome the beast in the brain. Work through your fears, and you will see it happen for you.

Be especially aware of anxiety-producing setups that can be avoided, if you anticipate them.

ᏋᏯᎧ

Setups.
It seems pretty obvious that you don't party all night or yell yourself hoarse at a game before you swim in a meet or sing a solo in church. People often don't think ahead and then it's too late. You open your mouth and nothing comes out but a croak. Your muscles feel tired and you can't clear your head.

As a performer, no matter what the venue you must enter a pact with yourself: *I will treat my body with care.* Guard your physical, mental and emotional well-being. They are just as important to a football player as they are to a dancer, singer, or comedian.

There are anxiety-producing setups that you can minimize if you recognize them beforehand. Setups are conditions you can find out ahead of time and try to control. Snares catch you unawares. Following are seven setups that often contribute to stage fright:

1. Insufficient preparation.
Lack of practice is the number one culprit on every anxiety list. We assume that if we are scared, it is because we didn't work hard enough. It goes without saying that you must be secure in your technique when you perform. But for those of us who battle the beast, no amount of technical preparation seems to deflect its subtle slings and arrows. Before you blame yourself, do a reality check.

Most people tend to be overly conscientious and overly practiced. This can lead us to tie ourselves into knots, just the setup we want to avoid as we go on stage. Remember how hard pianist Ignace Paderewski worked to be perfect, yet how terribly he suffered? Relax the day before, rather than pushing yourself to practice until the last minute.

Suppose you are asked to fill in for someone on the spur of the moment. There is hardly any time to prepare. Should you do it?

I think it depends entirely upon your feeling at that moment. Even if the play director pleads that without you there will be no performance, do not succumb if it goes against your better judgment. Know your limits. Do your knees turn to jelly when you aren't well rehearsed? Will you panic and forget your lines? We are all wired differently; we react to stress in very personal ways. If you suspect that appearing under these conditions won't do your reputation any favors, turn it down even if the performance has to be canceled. But if saving the day takes the pressure off your nerves, as it does for some people, give it a shot. I know performers who thrive in such emergency situations. There is no time for anxiety to build up—and *people are so incredibly grateful*! It's a wonderful way to earn some brownie points!

2. Boring material.

Another setup to be aware of as you practice is boring material. Everyone hates to work on something we find uninteresting or unappealing! If you need to do this, do not be tempted to work less carefully. A lack of mental engagement beforehand can give you a nerve jolt at performance time.

As a child, I had a hard time concentrating on piano pieces I didn't like. I slogged through assigned lessons because I assumed they were good for me. Worst of all were the ones in B flat with its two awkward black keys and clumsy fingering. It helped if I could find something good in the music and focus on that.

To avoid boredom and a sense of fatigue when practicing, one vocal coach suggested practicing the sections of performance material backwards. In other words, rehearse the last part first when you are fresh. In performance, they will be more energized. It may be merely psychological, but it works.

Performing material you genuinely don't care about can sometimes be an eye opener. I once won a piano competition I had entered to please my teacher. The prize was a solo appearance with a local orchestra. I played Cesar Franck's "Symphonic Variations" with an utter lack of concern. It was the first time that had ever happened to me, and I wondered about my lack of stage fright—especially since the piece was rather tricky in places. I realized that my life didn't depend upon how well I played the piano anymore; I had moved on to other things. Since then I try to recapture that sense of calm whenever nerves threaten to take over. I know that caring too much is a sign that something is out of balance, and I work to regain control.

3. Material that is too hard.
You are a violinist who has been invited to join a chamber music group. You show up at the first rehearsal ready and eager to make music. But after an hour you realize that this group likes to sight read through lots of pieces rather than work on one or two. This is not a challenge you enjoy; in fact, you hate scrambling for notes. Stress quickly replaces pleasure.

You consider your options. You can either hang on and try to develop better sight reading skills, or you can go with your feelings and quit before your nerves are totally shot. If you choose the latter course, you may grieve over the lost opportunity—but don't be too hard on yourself. Avoiding such a challenge is no reflection on your talent. People simply work differently.

Actors accept roles that stretch their capabilities, even if they know they are not quite up to it yet. What enterprising thespian will turn down the chance to play Willy Loman or Lady Macbeth? Singers, on the other hand, have to be

very careful not to overreach. They have only what baritone Sherrill Milnes has called "two little membranes"—
their fragile vocal chords—to work with. Singing too loud,
too high, too low or for too long strains them and can
do permanent damage. No tenor under the age of thirty
should sing Wagner's Siegfried or Tristan—in fact, most tenors should be wary of these heavy roles no matter how
enticing they are.

If you feel you aren't performing at the level you set for
yourself, you may be overreaching. Give the problematic
material a rest, no matter how much you love it. Put away
the heavy stuff until your technique is up to the demands it
makes. It is essential to build your career step by step on a
solid foundation. What's the hurry? You should be in prime
condition when you reach out for that cherished goal.

A word about the perfect recorded performances of
one's musical idol. It is common knowledge that recording
engineers use all kinds of technical tricks to achieve such
flawless results. A thrilling high C on a disk may not come
from that singer's throat at all. Often the best parts of several
tapings are strung together. Don't measure yourself against
unrealistic, even impossible, standards. Take time, focus on
your technique, listen to your body.

4. A teacher who is too demanding.
Madame Menova was the finest vocal coach in the Bay Area
She understood correct placement and proper breathing and
tailored her teaching to the needs of each student. She was
an excellent accompanist and a charming person, and she
showcased her students in opera previews geared to the San
Francisco Opera season. So why did most of her students
leave after a year or so?

I found out after I had studied with her for a few months. During the lesson Madame stopped to correct each poorly placed tone, each shallow breath, every weak attack. Her duty as she saw it was to address flaws on the spot. Madame was very thorough. Because there was always something to stop for, as time went on her students' ability to sing a song straight through without interruption deteriorated to the point where each impending performance brought on a massive attack of nerves. As I got to know them, I learned that most suffered the same anxiety I did. We couldn't shake the voice of Madame in our heads, criticizing every tone.

If this sounds familiar, if you leave each lesson feeling that you never do anything well enough, consider having a talk with your teacher. Tell Madame or Maestro that you would like to run through a piece without stopping even once, to get the feel of it. If he or she refuses, as happened to me with Madame—*that would be a waste of my time*, she said—then do it on your own as you practice, before your confidence is completely gone. Force yourself not to stop. Get a feeling for the mental or technical booby traps.

Rules about performing every note exactly as written are relatively recent in music history. The early composers reworked their material to suit individual performers and many versions exist. But during the nineteenth and twentieth centuries a rigid tradition grew, terrorizing generations of music students. If you didn't have a high C or couldn't master a particular cadenza, you couldn't perform the piece.

Today we have much greater artistic freedom. Singers often use transpositions in consultation with a conductor.[29] If a note or passage bothers you to the point of anxiety in a piece you have to perform, at least talk with your teacher about the possibility of altering it. What was forbidden forty years ago may not be so today.

Teachers sometimes unconsciously pass on to promising students their own unresolved career disappointments, frustrations and jealousies. This transfer can be so insidious that neither teacher nor student understands the real reason behind the unrelenting criticism. After all, isn't a teacher supposed to motivate a student to ever higher levels of perfection? Young people who adore their teachers are especially vulnerable to this kind of confidence battering that can end in serious stage fright problems. The more talented they are, the more they try to measure up, and the higher the unrelenting teacher raises the bar. The effect can be devastating.

Several New York-based voice teachers who had been famous Metropolitan Opera divas were notorious in this regard. One of them oozed disdain after a student's operatic debut. "Well, now we shall put that behind us," she said coldly at the next lesson. I was the young soprano, and I left feeling that in spite of good reviews I must have been a complete failure. Later I learned that one of her former students, a professional opera singer in Europe, had called the diva from Vienna to chastise her for having mentally abused her.

A good coach will develop your *performance skills*. That means your confidence in your talent as well as the technical details of your craft. You need the emotional strength to stand and deliver under sometimes enormous stress. There will be times when conductors, choreographers, coaches or directors will hammer away at your self-esteem. If "fight or flight" is all you have to work with, you cannot perform under pressure. You must develop a core of confidence that sustains you no matter what the circumstances. If your teacher cannot give you that, then leave, no matter how illustrious that teacher may be. Find a teacher or a program that can help you build up your inner equilibrium. Once that is established, you can always go back if you need your former teacher's special expertise. But enter the studio with your eyes wide open.

5. Feeling overwhelmed.

Singer Barbra Streisand has mentioned her panic fear of disappointing the thousands of people who paid for expensive tickets to hear her sing. Operatic soprano Maria Callas expressed the same anxiety. The weight of responsibility can become almost unbearable.

We all struggle, especially when we don't feel up to appearing on a particular day. The beast makes no distinction between amateur and professional. The fear of failure can be particularly hard on high-wire performers like operatic tenors and sopranos who are paid to produce a perfect high C every time. But we who are less famous can be just as terrified. *What if I have an accident on the way to the theater? What if I open my mouth and nothing comes out? What if I crack on the high note? What if my reed splits on the oboe solo? What if I faint on stage?*

What if, what if …?

If this happens to you, tell the beast to *be quiet*. Keep repeating this mantra quietly but firmly. Replace the voice in your head. The world will not end if you have a problem. Never underestimate the ingenuity of your colleagues to carry on, as illustrated in the following story recounted by Alec Baran:

> "An oboe player swallowed his reed just be-
> fore an orchestra concert and was waiting to
> be rushed to the hospital. The operator on the
> emergency line asked the conductor if he knew
> what to do. 'Yes,' said the conductor, we will use
> a muted trumpet.'"[30]

Emergencies happen all the time in the performing arts. On a college choir tour we had to work around non-functioning public address systems, missing piano keys, a power outage, vocal scores that were left behind in Nebraska on the way to Colorado, and three basses who fainted off the rear riser from the altitude change between Lincoln and Boulder. That evening the choir sang the whole program from memory for the first time, a remarkable achievement. It was a profound lesson in "carrying on" for all of us!

6. The material doesn't get to settle in.
You spend weeks rehearsing for a recital or a production that is over in just one night or a single weekend. You barely have gotten your sea legs. You would love to refine your performance, now that you know where the weak spots are. This happens over and over again, putting a strain on your nerves.

There are times when you are glad a performance is over and will never have to be repeated, such as a required exam scene in theater class or a tricky competition piece. But what if you really love the material?

I once attended a debut recital by a nervous soprano who forgot the words and had to start over several times during her opening group of Clara Schumann songs. The breathy, off-pitch sound was nothing like her normally clear voice. During the second group she managed to regained her composure and completed the recital successfully. Before the closing number she announced that after a short break, she would repeat the seldom-performed Schumann group for those who wished to stay. It was a courageous gesture and we appreciated hearing the songs again, this time sung well.

If you want another chance to perform your material, your community will have opportunities. Use your imagination. Which clubs, civic organizations, church groups, retirement communities, etc. look for programs? Neighboring towns may offer possibilities. Check the local paper for activities and contact information. Even events such as summer fairs and flea markets can be venues if you are into theatre or performance art. Whether you play an instrument or juggle or tell stories, someone will appreciate your offer.

7. Health issues.

Did you know that a health condition can bring on stage fright? Research links certain kinds of depression, phobias and panic attacks to underlying physical problems. B-vitamin deficiencies and biochemical imbalances affect the nervous system, and the stress of performing can trigger a variety of symptoms

Some people seem to need more of certain nutrients than other people. Maybe your body does not absorb B vitamins properly, or you may have a higher need for folic acid. Poor adrenal function and low blood sugar are two conditions that can bring on deep fatigue, so that a performance wipes you out. Inner ear problems can cause vertigo when you stand on risers or behind an elevated pulpit. Common allergies can cause anxiety in some people. Actress Helen Hayes was allergic to dust and was forced to end her stage career for this reason.

There is still much research to be done on these problems. If you suspect that something like this applies to you, surf the Web for the latest information on the link between nerves and body chemistry. To explore in depth, consult a certified specialist in nutritional medicine. Unfortunately, most general practitioners have only the most basic training in this field.

Always be on the alert for anything in your environment that could undermine your ability to perform at your best. Dust, cleaning solutions, perfumes, or animal dander can produce anxiety symptoms, to name a few of the culprits in our daily lives.

Some singers, actors and others who must use their voices have noticed symptoms like increased phlegm and hoarseness that appear after sitting in front of an older computer monitor for any length of time. If you suspect that a piece of equipment is affecting you. try to avoid long periods of exposure on the day of performance. If you can't do this, at least take frequent breaks.

Finally, you may notice that stress on the day of performance brings an increase in heartburn and acid reflux. This can produce hoarseness in your vocal cords. Carry a chewable antacid like Tums to calm your digestion and protect your voice. You can keep a step ahead of the inner beast if you anticipate it!

CHAPTER FIVE: CRUTCHES, ANCHORS, AND AUDITIONS

When you are just about to go on stage, the bladder strikes. Uncanny how that works. Visit the bathroom three times, and the urge hits again. Or waiting to go into an audition, your right leg starts to tremble visibly.

If you sit to give a talk your voice shakes. If you walk up and down, your knees threaten to give way. The beast is flexible. Hands sweat, bows tremble, muscles lock ...

The nervous system is inventive, and you may be sorely tempted to try whatever will make your symptoms go away. Maybe you use prescription tranquillizers or keep a pocket flask of vodka hidden in your briefcase. Just for a little while, until you get over the fear ...

But beware. There is a big difference between a crutch and an anchor.

A crutch is just a prop. You lean on it to jump-start you, either by dulling your nerves or revving them up, whichever you think you need. It is a temporary fix; it gets you out there, and that's about all it does. A crutch is a temporary measure, used and then discarded. Crutches do not build strength, they mask symptoms. As long as you depend on them, you will remain afraid. Crutches never build the personal strength in your core needed to tame anxiety.

An anchor, on the other hand, is a firm hold that won't weaken or make increasing demands over time. It is a permanent foundation—physical, mental, and emotional—that helps to overcome the effects of fear by strengthening your innermost core. Anchors become an integral part of you.

Let us examine both.

ᘿᗄ

Crutches.
Crutch 1. Uppers.
Uppers are stimulants like caffeine, sugar, cocaine and other drugs that get you going when you don't feel like doing anything. It could be the weather, or the time of the month, or too little sleep, or someone's negative vibes—whatever it is,

it overrides your preparation for an upcoming event, dampening your spirits and enthusiasm at a time when you need to be at your best, primed and ready.

Life happens. Some lucky people ride the crest of the waves no matter what happens to them. Others rise and fall with each situation. Stress drains them of energy, making it hard for them to pump themselves up on cue.

If you feel you have to resort to stimulants to get out of bed and off to the theater, be aware that you will pay a price. A chemically produced racing heartbeat leads to a lack of breath control and is not in your best interest. If you try to rationalize your artificially energized state—if you think that being wired and weird is part of your appeal—your hyped-up performance will probably be painful to watch.

Rick, a drummer friend, landed a touring gig with a popular rock group. At first he found being on the road exhilarating. But after a few months, the grinding boredom of long hauls on the bus got to him. Also, no one had warned him to pace himself. Traveling, performing and partying six nights a week left him so exhausted that he began to do cocaine just to get through the concerts. As a result, his playing became wilder and more erratic and he was fired.

Emma, an amateur opera singer, became nervously depressed before each performance. On principle she refused to take drugs, but she came to depend upon what she considered a harmless stimulant: an aspirin dissolved in a glass of Coca Cola©. But as time went on its effects waned, as often happens with stimulants, and because of overuse she developed heart problems that ended her career.

These are only two examples of many ways people become dependent upon destructive crutches when there are healthy and effective alternatives available. Emma could have taken a brisk walk that would have stimulated her brain circulation and brought a sense of well-being. If Rick had asked more seasoned members of the band for advice on how to avoid burnout, he would have learned that those with longevity avoided the partying, got plenty of sleep, and took up a hobby such as photography to make productive use of time on the road.

Relying on excessive use of stimulants is especially tragic for successful performers. Talk about pressure! They must be at the top of their game every time they go on. Unfortunately, overmedicating usually brings on the result they fear the most: sloppiness and uninspiring appearances that if repeated too often bring down careers. Why risk destroying your dream?

Many people think alcohol and nicotine are uppers. In fact they are the opposite. They are depressants. Alcohol slows reaction time and dulls reality. Smoking clouds your brain, diminishes lung power and produces a breathy, reduced vocal range, hardly the way to enhance a budding career unless you are going for that kind of an effect.

Dancers are among the performers who need the highest physical control on stage. For a quick picker-upper, they have found that the least harmful stimulant, according to former Pacific Northwest Ballet star Linnette Roe, is caffeine because it has the least harmful effect on performance.[31] Dr. Richard Gibbs, the San Francisco Ballet's physician, agrees that recreational drugs like cocaine are so destructive to performance that dancers seldom use them. "I'm with the dancers several days each week," says Gibbs, "and I never see behavior, hyperactivity, glazed eyes, dilated pupils or other physical signs of drug use."[32]

Chemical uppers do not improve your inherent ability. No drug, steroid or stimulant will give extra resonance to an actor's voice or add emotional oomph to a song. They may delude you into thinking so, and you are likely to appear more foolish than profound. If you need a stimulant to get going, emulate the dancers and stick to a cup of coffee or tea.

Crutch 2. Downers.
Downers are depressors. Crutches like alcohol, cigarettes, and narcotic drugs can leave you drowsy and sluggish. As they dull your sense of reality, you will be unaware that you are

performing poorly. The best that can be said about downers is that they do keep you from fleeing the stage.

Alcohol is especially deceptive because, as mentioned above, it masquerades as an upper. You may think that after a few drinks you have become relaxed and scintillating when in fact you are over-reactive and slower at the same time. *Modern Drummer* magazine warns band musicians against the tendency to drink themselves into boring, sloppy, repetitive playing.[33] Richard Burton's sloshed stage appearances became an embarrassment toward the end of a long and legendary career. Do you want to end that way?

While the thought of performing can tie us into knots, we must think of the consequences before popping tranquilizers or puffing a joint. Consider the following offstage encounter reported by performer-composer Michael Colgrass:

> "Once I was waiting backstage to perform along with another musician, and, to my amazement, she pulled out a little silver box, extracted a marijuana cigarette, and lit up. When I asked her if smoking dope before going on stage was advisable she said: 'Oh, I always do it. I think playing should be a special experience for the performer and then that feeling carries over to the audience.'
>
> "She was right. The audience almost fell asleep..."[34]

This performer exchanged a natural sense of excitement and awareness for an artificial state of consciousness in a mistaken attempt to reach her audience. I suspect that she did not trust her ability enough and responded by retreating from reality. We are all insecure when we expose ourselves to others. But should we answer the fight-or-flight challenge by dulling ourselves? I hardly think so. Who benefits from this? Certainly not the audience. The goal is, after all, to give the best and most engaging performance possible.

Singer Liza Minelli fought performance panic with a variety of uppers and downers throughout her career. She had started out with good intentions;. In an early interview she said that she would rather be frightened on stage and know she is really alive, than be dulled with drugs. After watching her mother Judy Garland struggle against intense fear, Minelli had resolved not to get caught in addiction. But performing was never easy for her, either, and as each appearance continued to be a challenge she had to fight the beast over and over again.

Crutch 3. Beta blockers.
Beta-blocker drugs like atenolol or propranolol are used in small amounts by many performers. They are neither uppers nor downers. Originally developed to control high blood pressure, it was discovered that beta blockers had a welcome side effect for performers: they reduced stage fright without a significant reduction in ability.

Beta blockers work by inhibiting the production of adrenaline. Now, we know that a little adrenaline is good because it adds an extra sparkle to performance. Here again we have the example of dancers to inspire us. A survey by *Dance Magazine* found that although forty percent of respondents suffered from stage fright, many dancers said they avoid beta blockers because they want the extra nervous edge.[35]

But most of us have real problems with the sweaty palms, racing heartbeat, lack of breath and other physical handicaps that excess adrenaline produces. Beta blockers lessen these symptoms. While you may still feel anxious, you are spared the shaky voice and wobbly knees. A violinist plays in public for the first time without a trembling bow arm; a flutist possesses a steady tone and long breath. What wonderful relief!

Of the calming drugs available, a low-dosage beta blocker is usually considered the least detrimental to performance. But it is not for everyone. "In terms of the athletic population, beta-blockers have adverse consequences," says Donald J. Rose, founding director of the Harkness Center for Dance Injuries in Manhattan.[36] He maintains that they can reduce stamina and may have dangerous side effects such as severe asthma attacks. Thus they must always be used under a doctor's supervision.

Every crutch, whether a stimulant or depressant, should be temporary. Your goal is to develop enough personal strength to neutralize the forces that produce debilitating symptoms without the use of external aids. If you have a broken leg, you don't live the rest of your life in a wheelchair or leaning on a crutch. You eventually discard them as your leg bears its own weight. It is the same with performing. You want to develop effective techniques that strengthen your body's own energies and resources. That is the goal of all healing.

☯

Anchors.
When you are firmly anchored, you have control over mind, body and spirit. You discipline your breathing; you exercise to stimulate brain circulation; you learn relaxation and meditation techniques. And all along the way, you practice/practice/practice! That is the iron foundation on which you anchor your talent and your performance ability so that the physical symptoms of anxiety no longer threaten your composure.

Anchor 1. Correct breathing.
No matter what the field is—singing, dancing, acting, speaking, comedy, baseball, juggling, impromptu praying—to be in control of your body, you need the full use of your breathing mechanism.

Italian tenor Luciano Pavarotti found this out when he discovered that he was not maintaining sufficient vocal control when he didn't feel well. In a PBS documentary on his life and career, he says that soprano Joan Sutherland suggested he needed to strengthen his breath support and helped him improve it.

Anxiety causes erratic breathing. But anxiety can also be triggered by breathing habits in normal daily life that unconsciously constrict the lungs, starving the body of oxygen and thereby arousing a sense of unease.

Most people don't think about how they breathe unless they are afflicted with asthma or emphysema. We take this bodily function for granted. After all, it's automatic. Haven't we done it since we were born? What is there to know?

Plenty. Doctors tell us that your lungs are the laziest organs in the body. Most adults are quite happy to be lazy, shallow breathers, but we were not born that way. Watch a sleeping baby; see how its little diaphragm expands and contracts automatically with each breath. Its lungs expand fully like internal balloons. By the time we go to school, however, most of us lose the breathing technique we were born with. We no longer expand our lungs completely the way we did as infants. Under the stresses of life our breathing reacts to emotion and becomes shallow, constricted, irregular. The result can be a gnawing sense of unease—nature's way of saying: *pay attention to me!*

People who feel frustrated may overbreathe or even hyperventilate to the point of fainting. To reestablish the oxygen/carbon dioxide ratio in their bodies, they breathe into a paper bag. Other individuals under stress hold their breath until they become dizzy. Angry toddlers can turn blue from oxygen deprivation. Adults sitting in a doctor's waiting room may experience feelings of vertigo without knowing why.

Do a test on a normal day. Monitor yourself; jot down when and how your breathing changes. Is it different when you talk to your child, your mom, your boss, your spouse, your teacher, your colleague? How was it different? Did you hold your breath? Breathe faster? Tighten your chest and shoulders? Take short, shallow puffs? Did you sigh or take big, deep-down breaths? (Had you stopped breathing?) Become aware of which people and situations affect you most. Then try to exercise your favorite breathing technique to relax when talking with them.

Unless you have had training with a breathing coach, your chest probably moves up and down when you breathe in and out. This is a sign that you are not using the full capacity of your lungs. For performance purposes and to gain control of anxiety symptoms, you must learn to breathe as a baby does.

In former times, opera singers strengthened their diaphragm muscles by breathing in against the round end of a grand piano. You can get the same effect with a package of small party balloons. Make sure they are the little ones! Try to blow each one up in one breath. Not easy! You have to activate your diaphragm to do it. Blow until you feel the muscle move and the balloon expands. You may get dizzy at first from the effort, but keep at it.

Full lung expansion exercise.
1. Stand or sit up straight. Place the palm of one hand in the middle of your stomach below the rib cage. just above your belly button.

Take a few deep breaths. Does your chest heave? If so, take slow breaths and try to breathe against your palm. Keep your chest still. When you feel movement against your palm, you are using the diaphragm muscle. Practice breathing in and out against your palm until it becomes second nature and your chest remains still.

2. When you have mastered the above, put your palms on your sides below the rib cage and try to breathe out against them. When you feel your sides move outward against your palms, you are breathing properly from the diaphragm. Practice this until it becomes second nature and your chest remains still.

Continue checking your front and side breathing until both become your normal pattern.

3. Now it gets hard!
Place one hand on your back against your spine at waist level. While breathing in, try to push against your back hand. At first you won't notice movement; keep trying until you feel your back rib cage expand outward. If it makes you a bit dizzy, this is normal. Practice this until it becomes second nature and your chest remains still.

4. Continue checking your breathing until expanding and contracting your diaphragm becomes your normal mode of breathing. Blow up more small balloons (new ones!) once in a while to keep yourself in shape.

Deep breathing is the first step to breath control. The second step—especially vital for singers, speakers and actors—is learning to keep chest and rib cage fully supported with the diaphragm muscle in a strong, open position as you sing or speak. This can be difficult if you perform in a sitting position; your body will tend to slouch. But make this your default breathing in real life so it becomes normal. Along with your technical proficiency, it will be your strongest anchor.

Anchor 2. Relaxation techniques.
Thousands of books, articles and seminars are available on a wide range of relaxation techniques. They explore every angle of the subject from the Alexander Technique to Zen. You can find them all on the Internet, Both Alexander and Zen, by the way, have helped a lot of stressed-out people.

It would be nice if there were a relaxation technique that works for everyone. But there isn't. Stress is a lifelong battle with very personal, different roadblocks. Many are rooted in long-buried memories and unresolved emotions. What helps you is all that matters. Which approach speaks to you in a positive way? What will strengthen your core in mind, body and spirit?

Although there is no one answer for all of us, the following basic breathing exercise is a quick way to calm anxiety-driven erratic breathing and a rapid heartbeat.

Basic breathing exercise.
1. Take two quick shallow breaths to start.
2. Inhale slowly while counting to five.
3. Exhale slowly, lips slightly parted, counting to   ten.
4. Repeat steps 2 and 3 five times;
5. End with one normal deep breath.
Caution: Don't do this exercise more than five times at once, or you may become dizzy!

You can do this exercise anywhere—on the bus, sitting in traffic, at your desk, on the sports field, and just before you "go on." This exercise keeps enough carbon dioxide in your system to help quiet your thoughts. There is evidence that the effect is similar to the relaxation smokers feel when they inhale, but without the bad effects.

The following exercise is done on the floor in a quiet room.

Full body relaxation exercise.
1. Sit comfortably or lie down flat on the floor (not on a bed) with your legs together and your arms at your sides. Close your eyes and clear your mind of thoughts. You want to concentrate on your feelings.

2. Eyes closed, visualize the top of your head Tell your brain to relax. Visualize the empty space behind your eyes and nose;

your sinus cavities. Relax your forehead muscles; release the tension between your eyes.

Relax your ears, your mouth, throat, tongue and chin. Let your jaw go slack.

3. Now, visualize slowly down your body, dwelling for thirty seconds on each part:

    neck,

    shoulders,

    chest,

    arms,

    abdomen

    buttocks,

    thighs,

    calves,

    feet,

    toes.

Don't rush. By the time you reach your toes, your breathing should be slow and steady, your body relaxed and your mind at peace.

This exercise can be done the other way around if you prefer. Starting at your toes, visualize and relax each part of your body up to the top of your head. Some people feel that their negative energy is more effectively released that way. Do what works best for you.

Red balloon exercise.
This meditation exercise, a version of a Chinese visualization technique, has been used by Beverly Wideman in classes at New York University's Tisch School of the Arts graduate acting program. Wideman's students call it the Red Balloon Exercise. It is a good companion to the Full Body Exercise.

1. Sit comfortably or lie flat in a relaxed position with your eyes closed. Visualize either one large red balloon or lots of small red balloons, whichever you prefer. The red color is important because it symbolizes negative energy.

2. As you bring up each worry and negative thought, blow it with a "puff" into the large balloon or each individual one. When you are finished, release the balloons. Let them drift upwards toward the ceiling.

3. Now do one of the following three things:
    a. let the balloons rest at the ceiling for future action;
    b. bring one or more of them down, one at a time, and resolve the   issue;
    c. pop them.

Wideman's students say they usually end up popping all their balloons.

Anchor 3. Symptom substitution.
Earlier we heard about Ron the pianist whose symptoms migrated to his throat when he began singing. His hands didn't sweat anymore, but his mouth dried up. Is it possible to divert symptoms so they don't affect your performance?

Yes, it is possible with a little practice; call it mind over matter. The first thing is to be alert for such symptoms. I once watched a baritone sing a group of German Lieder on a television program. During the first song the camera concentrated on his face and upper body, and the soloist projected a calm, confident manner. But in the middle of the second song the camera panned back, revealing that the singer's left-hand fingers were wiggling frantically back and forth. The effect was mesmerizing; it was hard to concentrate on the beautiful singing. This artist, or his manager, could not have been aware of this habit or they would have warned the cameraman that he released tension in this way.

Lecturers with wobbly knees can direct the tension farther down by wiggling their toes in their shoes. Actors clench and unclench their toes on stage. But use this method only if you are wearing shoes! After a barefoot performance of the play "Oedipus," actor Laurence Olivier was taken aside by his friend Alfred Lunt and told, "I was fascinated by your feet; the more intense you got, the more rigidly did your big toes stand straight up in the air!" Horrified, Olivier analyzed his walk and discovered a new way to step that fixed the problem and it became part of his characterization.[37]

Remember, tension has to go somewhere. Olivier had to struggle with the problem of releasing it throughout his long career. As a budding young actor he had a habit of giggling on stage that he could not shake for years; he was once fired for it. Playwright Noël Coward helped him finally to overcome this urge during the first run of Coward's Broadway play "Private Lives." The author/director privately told the cast members to make Olivier giggle on stage at every opportunity. Afterwards Coward would assemble the cast and crew and bawl out the actor publicly for giving in to what Coward called "this amateurish smear." It took nine months, but the shame therapy worked. His inner discipline took over and Olivier was cured.[38]

Anchor 4. Ritual behavior.
An actress friend of mine always carries a heavy gold coin imprinted with the name and picture of a luxury hotel in Hawaii. She rubs this coin between her fingers before every entrance. It is a harmless way to shore up her confidence and a feeling of success that calms her nerves when she goes on.

Operatic soprano Rosa Ponselle had to walk around the block several times to work up the courage to enter the theater. She also required all the windows backstage and in her dressing room to be flung wide open, winter or summer, for two hours before each performance.[39]

A German singer named von zur Muehlen always sang with one foot resting on a horseshoe.[40]

Ritual behaviors can provide you with a sense of security when you most need it. As children we took comfort from hugging a beloved blanket or stuffed toy. Grownups have the same need at times. Fingering a precious object helps many of us get through nerve-wracking situations. So don't feel shy about carrying a special piece of jewelry, coin, lucky handkerchief or religious symbol that helps you to focus your mind.

If your talisman or pre-performance ritual seems like superstition to other people—if they tease you for taking only one route to the theatre or for turning around three times before going on stage—so what? Smile and ignore the comments.

But guard against relying too much on a ritual. If something becomes an obsession—you would go to pieces if you had to perform without it—the beast in your brain has taken control and you need to deal with that. Like the youth in Salt Lake City who couldn't leave his room until he touched the doorknob 375 times,[41] you can become a slave to your panic. Rituals exist to serve you, and not the other way around!

Prayer is one of the most effective forms of ritual behavior for those who are afraid to face the limelight. Whatever your connection to a higher power may be, use it. Let prayer, a psalm, a bible passage or a personal mantra help center your thoughts as you wait to go on. Let your mind quiet down. You will quiet your breathing as well. And disciplined breathing is the ultimate anxiety control for all performers.

☙❧

Auditions.

One of the hardest tests for those who live with performance anxiety is auditioning. So much seems to ride on each one! More than a few talented performers, as well as people in the business world who fear job interviews, have passed up opportunities to grow because of the audition hurdle.

Casting director Michael Shurtleff knows all about the extreme edginess of actors who can barely control their fears under normal circumstances, let alone under the stress of an audition. Such fears, he maintains, often rest on traumatic childhood experiences that undergird the craft of acting. He recalls walking with an actor friend in the country one night in the dark when a branch touched his friend's face and the actor let out a scream. Later, thinking about his friend's trigger-finger fright response, Shurtleff realized that many actors live on an emotional razor's edge. "They scream inside," he says vividly, "filled with horror at the sadistic audition situation that might accidentally touch a branch across the face."[42]

Tenor Robert Mitchell sang for many years in and around New York City, in principal roles with the Amato Opera Company and in other venues. His candid memoir *Opera Inside Out* describes what can only be called his audition from hell, which happened at the height of his career in the fabled Metropolitan Opera house (the Met).

Mitchell prepared carefully for his big chance. The audition was a surprise, arranged by an acquaintance with connections. Mitchell knew he had a tendency to fall ill before important performances, but he thought he was safe because it was the middle of August, and he never got sick in the summer. Yet—a few days beforehand, he came down with the flu. Giddy with fever and feeling weak, he dragged himself out of bed and went to the theater.

He was waved into a waiting area by a guard who crossed his name off a list. Crowds of people were milling around, hustling to and fro, in and out of closed doors, or chatting in blue cushioned chairs. He managed to grab one of the chairs and sank into it, already exhausted and wondering if he should have come, yet not wanting to abandon what could be his only shot at the Met.

When his name was called, he was taken in an elevator down several floors below street level to the bowels of the building. He stepped out into a freezing, air-conditioned hallway and found one chair that faced a large closed double door. At first he was alone. Then two fashionable women alit from the elevator, breezed by him and were welcomed into the room with effusive greetings. One of the women he recognized as a famous mezzo-soprano. The other was probably a student of hers. Soon he heard what sounded like a lovely voice singing an aria. Then he heard a second aria, and a third.

As the women left, again with effusive words all around, he went to the door and entered what he describes as a frigid vault. The temperature hitting his body caused him to break out into a cold sweat. On the other side of the large room sat three men at a long table, and an accompanist at a piano. Ignoring him, they continued conversing among themselves about how good the mezzo-soprano looked. After waiting in vain for a signal to approach, he walked over to the piano and gave his music to the accompanist. He continues in his own words:

> "Suddenly they stop talking and look at me with fierce eyes, as if to say, 'So what are you standing there for? Sing already!' They still had not spoken a word to me. I say something to the effect

that we were just waiting for them. They give me a face that says, 'Just who in the bloody blazes do you think YOU are?'"[43]

He began to sing. He had tried to warm up at home before he left, but it felt so terrible that he stopped. Now, at the moment he had anticipated for most of his adult life, his hard-won confidence deserted him. All the doubts and uncertainties he had battled. for so long took over:

> "Immediately I know I am in trouble. My voice is cold—in every sense of the word. When I am not properly warmed up and try to sing in full voice, my voice is pale and labored and probably under the pitch. I can neither feel it nor hear it properly. I get hoarse very quickly. ... By the end of the aria I'm really struggling, and the guys are back to talking among themselves again.
>
> "I stop singing. They keep talking—as if I weren't there. ... At last one of them looks over to me as if to say, 'Are *you* still here?' ... They resume talking. I turn to the accompanist, thank him as I pick up my music. ... I turn and leave. ... I never auditioned for the Met again."[44]

Auditions can arouse emotions that lie buried deep within us. The origins of old fears about ourselves are usually lost, but the beast in our brain knows where they are and how to reactivate them. And they can sabotage us if we do not work to tame them.

I have described Robert Mitchell's experience in some detail because there is a lot that can be learned from it. First of all, the glamorous fantasies we hold in our heads about the world of performance are just that: fantasies. Scratch the surface at the Met, and you will find the same hard realities that afflict every field of endeavor. Second, pure talent is not enough. To get inside; much depends upon who guards the gate. Find out as much as you can ahead of time about the people running the production and what they are looking for. Third, never let your life depend upon those three minutes. If you care too much, chances are that your nerve will fail, and with it your physical control. Remember: *There will be other "three minutes."* Pick yourself up, dust yourself off, and try again—and again.

Andrea, an actress, approached her first New York auditions with great trepidation; not knowing what to expect aroused intense anxiety in her. But after answering a few audition calls and talking with other actors, she realized that being chosen for a part had little to do with her training or resume. She either had the right look or she didn't. Since they were all in the same boat, the other actors were generally helpful rather than competitive, trading tips on upcoming shows, and this greatly eased her anxiety.

When fear surfaces at an audition, ask yourself: *What is the worst thing that could happen to me?* You will probably think one of three things:

— I will disgrace myself;

— I won't get the coveted part;

— I'll never get any part.

One method that works for many people is to close your eyes and visualize a frightening situation that is worse than what you will face when you are called in. For example, the fantasy I often imagined was a scene from a movie: a jumbo jet nearly out of fuel flies low over the Pacific into the sunset, lost, not knowing how far it is from the nearest landing strip. For me, it doesn't get any scarier than that! I let myself feel the panic of a passenger in that plane gliding just above the ocean. Then, when I open my eyes, I am so relieved to be back in the audition reality that the performing fear subsides.

Find out what works for you. But always try to calm your breathing, using the exercises in this manual. If you want to mentally review your audition material, go over it slowly. *Do not allow your mind to race!* Engage in conversation with others only if it helps to distract you.

Finally, never allow the beast to draw you into fears about a failure that hasn't happened. Keep your mind in the present moment: *I am sitting on a chair outside a closed door with a lot of other people. Pedestrians go about their daily business outside on the sidewalk. It's just another day for them. So it is for me.*

And I am going to be fine.

CHAPTER SIX: FIRST AID

First aid can be used to correct habits and mannerisms that are not directly related to your performing craft but cause unnecessary tension. They do not usually require major psychic surgery—thus the term first aid—but can easily be corrected with awareness and a little determination. You may have a habit, for example, of holding your breath when your supervisor talks to you at work. Or perhaps you hold tension in your shoulders when you stand in front of people. Then you wonder why you always get a headache on these occasions. By recognizing and redirecting such tension-producing habits, you will help your body perform more effectively.

While modifying old behavior is possible for all of us, we have to be willing to change it. If everyone in your family avoided shaking hands with strangers and you cannot even bring yourself to "pass the peace" in church, you may have an anxiety problem as a lecturer, If you become nervous when forced to make small talk because at home no one talked much and you don't know how, your brain may freeze up whenever you have to sit through a banquet dinner and you will avoid such appearances.

These may seem like peripheral issues But they can add stress when you must appear in public. And ethnic patterns differ. Direct eye contact is considered aggressive in some cultures; in others, a lack of eye contact is a sign of shiftiness or disapproval. Your reaction to body language can provoke unconscious anxiety and tension if it is left unexamined., and you certainly do not need the added pressure in the diverse world of performance.

I was raised in a family that did not express their affection in outward physical ways; it was not part of the old German cultural pattern. Thus, as an adult when I lived for a time in Argentina, it was hard for me to exchange kiss-on-both-cheeks greetings from male and female friends. I felt a kind of stage fright every time we had to attend social functions. Gradually I got over my old inhibitions after constant exposure to the culture, and a lot of whispered prayers. Today kisses of greeting are routine everywhere, but most of us will encounter similar cultural shocks at one time or another.

Take a close look at your family background. Is there something besides normal performance adrenalin that may be affecting your nerves? Do you dislike the physicality with which people greet each other backstage or in the green room? Do you dread making small talk? Are you afraid to speak up about conditions that bother you? Let us look at a few common issues a little more closely.

❦

Shyness.
In the Pennsylvania Dutch mountain church that my husband pastored for many years, men did not talk much. They left that to the women. The men worked hard, fathered large families, and looked after their kinfolk, but they spoke only when they thought it was necessary, which was not often. Sit beside one of them at a church picnic, and you might as well be sitting alone. Yet on Sunday mornings they would sing the hymns lustily, often in parts, as their fathers had done before them..

By contrast, the men at a pastorate in New York City had no problem making small talk and voicing their opinions in meetings, but when it came to singing, their lips barely moved even when the hymn was as familiar as "Amazing Grace."

We all carry learned behaviors around with us. If dad talks a blue streak at the dinner table but barely mumbles in church, that's how his sons will probably act. The reverse is sometimes true as well, especially during the rebellious years. Both are likely to be embarrassed by parents they think sing too loudly, and take pains not to imitate them, but are not shy about screaming into a garage-band mike.

We are not always aware of the roots of our behavior. Some of us may simply have been born shy. But others retreat into a shell when as children they are ridiculed by their peers—for ill-fitting clothes, or geeky hair, or getting good grades, or lugging a violin. The last thing they want is to draw attention to themselves.

Yet performers have a talent or a message we very much want to share. How can we rid ourselves of voices from the past that feed the inner beast.? *You're weird! You think you're special or something? You're nobody,* etc. Wounding words at a vulnerable age are hard to forget. Yet, amazingly, many shy people find their voices on stage or in the pulpit. Once they gain the courage to enter the glare of the spotlight, a feeling of liberation can fill them in a way that anxiety sufferers can only envy. Such people blossom in the limelight like flowers unfolding, and it is beautiful to see.

While actors have a particular reputation for this kind of dual persona, a surprising number of pastors and public speakers are the same way. They seem distant and shy in social situations, yet before an audience they project an outgoing, confident image.

Making small talk backstage, in the green room or at a conference dinner can be torture for shy people waiting to "go on." You may become nauseous or even avoid such engagements because of your fears. But don't give in without a fight! There are ways to get through such daunting situations.

The most important point is to realize that most superficial conversations are not about you at all; they are about the other person. So program into your handheld device or on a slip of paper some general phrases or questions you can use with any stranger, preferably questions that cannot be answered with yes or no. Begin by introducing yourself:

Hi, I'm [Kerry Smith], and you are —?

What can you tell me about this group/event/program?

As you listen to the answer, be alert for a "hook," something that can lead you to ask another question. For example: *You say that this group raises funds for [name of organizations]?How did you get started? You work for Raymour and Flanigan? Where does all that furniture come from? You've belonged to this club for how long? What got you to join? What kept you interested?* etc. etc.

It takes a little practice, but before you know it, you won't be nervous anymore because your mind will be occupied. *Don't worry about the impression you are making.* That will take care of itself. If you concentrate on getting to know him/her, you will be remembered as good company!

A music sorority in my college held "rush" teas to get to know all the new female music students. While they helped us meet the freshmen, these get-acquainted events forced us to acquire social skills most of us had not learned at home, such as making small talk with strangers in social situations. To do this, we combined a list of generic questions with a method of planned circulating that enabled every group member to talk to each new student. We each followed a designated person around the room. As my partner left a group or a person, I wandered over and struck up a conversation in her place. The person following me took my former spot. It was a fun way to circulate because it was not about us but about getting to know the new freshmen, and that took away the nervous edge. I have always been grateful for having had that practice.

If your shyness around strangers intensifies your nervousness when you have to perform, try this method with a friend at a party. Follow your friend around the room, but joining it. Your friend would remain long enough to bring you into the conversation or fill you in about the person or persons, then excuse her/himself after a few minutes. You just listen if that feels more comfortable, or engage the person next to you, practicing your questions and listening for hooks. After a little while, wave to an unseen acquaintance, excuse yourself (*I'm sorry, will you excuse me?*) and move on.

Remember: Do not talk about yourself unless the person asks. Concentrate on the clues you are picking up from them. Your goal is to practice small talk, not impress. You should be so focused that you won't have time to be concerned about what they think of you. If you do meet a person who seems genuinely interested in you, congratulations! Unless they are playing the same game you are, you have hit the jackpot.

ʘɞ

Low tolerance level.
Nothing is more difficult for an anxiety-prone person with a short fuse than to avoid lashing out when someone jabbers backstage or in the green room before a performance or at rehearsal. They are probably just releasing their own nervous energy, but anger rises in you because the last thing you want when you are trying to stay calm and focused is someone talking into your ear. You may overreact because a costume doesn't fit, or when a prop isn't where it should be on stage.

You know from experience that blowing off steam in public is counterproductive, but you can't help it. That's how you were raised. Your dad taught you not to suffer fools gladly. People in your family let it out when something irritated them. Isn't it better to get things off your chest?

Not if you want to build a performing career in the real world. You need to find a better way to handle frustration Unless you are a superstar who brings in big bucks, you cannot alienate cast and crew and expect to be hired again.

Avoiding trigger reactions at rehearsals or before going on stage is a matter of learning how to handle an adrenalin rush, an important discipline if you want to control performance nerves. After the first flash of irritation at someone or something, take three immediate steps: a) acknowledge the signs (rush of anger, flushing face); b) physically step back from the offender; and c) take several quick breaths to slow the coursing adrenalin in your body. Then devise a measured response that will not disrupt your pre-performance state of mind.

If you want to be left alone, arrive with two thoughts in mind: I will avoid eye contact with anyone, and I will make myself scarce. After waving a friendly "Hi, everybody," disappear into an out-of-the-way corner in the wings or among the stored scenery, preferably a dimly lit spot. If you have to endure makeup, close your eyes and grunt answers to discourage conversation. If a chatterbox targets you, smile briefly, get busy with your score or script and ignore them. If they persist, retreat to a restroom stall for a few minutes and do the Basic Breathing Exercise described above.

Situations are bound to arise that force you to interact with people in an unfamiliar or unpleasant way. At the end of such days you will collapse on your bed mentally exhausted. Challenge yourself to work through the experience. Spend half an hour alone in your room. Take off your shoes, loosen your belt, stretch out on the floor, close your eyes, and do the Red Balloon Exercise:

—visualize the persons or events that challenged your patience (take your time; do it slowly);

—puff each frustration into an imaginary red balloon (remember that the color red symbolizes negative energy);

—let the accumulated frustrations float up to the ceiling. In your mind, visualize them hanging up there. Think about how you might deal better with them if they happen again. Take your time.

—When you are ready, bring the balloon back down to you—and pop it.

ᘂᕀᘁ

Tension mannerism control.

We all do things to release stress when we are bored, uncertain, irritated or anxious in daily life. We drum the table, tap a foot, clench and unclench our fists. Such actions are usually unconscious, but they can be distracting to an audience, as happened when Laurence Olivier's rigid big toes betrayed his tension.

To find out if you have habits you might not be aware of, ask a trusted friend to watch you. If possible, film yourself in action. You cannot divert tension if you don't know there is a problem. Check for the following common mannerisms:

— "Video-game thumb" (your thumbs stick straight up while you are speaking or singing). *Keep your thumbs pressed into your palms.*

— Raising and lowering eyebrows. *(Practice with a piece of tape across your forehead.)*

— Constant blinking. *(Practice staring; rehearse in front of a mirror).*

— Rocking sideways or back and forth. *(Arrange a signal with a friend in the audience.)*

— Drumming fingers on a conference table. *(Keep your hands off the table.)*

— Waving hands when speaking. *(Practice with a friend holding them still, to get the feeling.)*

— Licking your lips. *(Press the tip of your tongue against the inside of your lower teeth to control the reflex.)*

— Clenched fists. *(Let the fingers of both hands lightly touch each other.)*

— The urge to swallow without saliva. *(A closed-mouth yawn relaxes the jaw and throat.)*

— Constant repetitious words or phrases—"ya know," like," "right?"—when you give a talk or interview..*(Listen to yourself or have a friend monitor you. Practice not using the words in normal conversation. Close your mouth briefly when the urge comes.)*

੧੭

Aches and pains.
Another example of behavior that can trigger stress is an exaggerated fear of the aches, pains and cold symptoms that hit out of the blue when a performance is coming up. I am not talking about real health issues; people who perform in spite of painful physical handicaps are amazing to me. That takes courage

and resilience! I am thinking of the excuses some people use as a reason not to show up for rehearsal when they don't feel their best, or the litany of woes that others who do show up inflict on the rest of the cast. Such behavior adds stress to the nervous tension surrounding everyone in any production. Frequently pleading illness can be a thinly disguised cry for sympathy fueled by unrealistic standards of perfection.

At the risk of sounding like a broken record, I want to repeat that the way we respond to life's challenges is strongly conditioned by our upbringing. Did your working mother always call in sick when she had a headache? Did your dad only carry out household chores when he felt like it? Were you kept home from school if you so much as complained of a bellyache? Such early patterns are not written in stone. If you find that the way you grew up was more self-indulgent than the highly competitive performing world will allow, you can and should modify your behavior with a little will power and self-awareness.

I once was in a production with a soprano who only showed up for half the rehearsals. She always seemed to be coming down with something. It took coaxing telephone calls from the rest of us to bring her in, and when she was there she dampened everyone's spirits by complaining about how bad she felt. I suspected that she thrived on the attention. My suspicion was confirmed when she told the director that she was not up to appearing that night in her opera scene. Out of patience, the director assigned another soprano to her part and within the hour she had miraculously recovered. This promising young singer with a beautiful high C never managed to realize her career potential.

We absorb all kinds of signals as we grow up. As adults we have the gift of hindsight, and unfortunately not all of us use it. If you skip rehearsal because you are tired or just don't feel like it, what is your inner voice telling you? Be honest. Are you unconsciously imitating Mom and Dad? Or does the thought of performing under less than perfect conditions frighten you to the point of actual illness? If the latter is true, why do you feel that kind of pressure?

Perfection is an unrealistic expectation. Every seasoned performer knows that. We are never as good "out there" as we are in the resonant privacy of a practice room. The best we can achieve under most circumstances is sixty or seventy percent on a personal perfection scale. We have to make our peace with that. It is a reality we all share.

Do not let a normal headache or a hangover become an excuse for skipping rehearsal. If you can walk and talk and are not contagious, make the effort. Remember that half the world's work is done by people who don't feel well. And the other half didn't feel well yesterday!

We all heard the stories about how our forebears slogged through miles of snow to attend school. In those days there were no excuses to stay home. If you didn't have a fever, you went. This tradition served many performers well. I think of operatic baritone Sherrill Milnes, who grew up on a farm and prided himself on singing hundreds of performances without canceling. Milnes was no healthier than other baritones, but his upbringing in rural Illinois taught him that no matter how he felt, he could see it through.

Word travels fast in the business. Those who have a reputation for being dependable are the first to be called. When director Martin Scorsese was asked in a television interview why he liked to use actor Alec Baldwin, he said that in addition to his formidable talent, Baldwin was dependable and arrived prepared.

Of course it is hard to drag yourself to rehearsal or a presentation with a fractured ankle, wearing that awful black boot. But knowing you can function anyhow brings an added sense of confidence that can reduce your anxiety. So make the drill part of your being: if you sign on, you show up!

CHAPTER SEVEN: PURIST TRADITION

To use or not to use a score?

In chapter one we saw how Professor Lange could not complete his recital because he had developed a fear of forgetting the music. The following year his program consisted of two piano concertos. He had two grand pianos placed side by side on the stage, and an advanced student played the orchestra part on the second piano. Both of them used scores and had page turners at their side. The program went very well and the audience responded with enthusiastic applause. From then until his retirement, Professor Lange performed his annual obligation with a score.

Whether you use music, manuscript, notes, or perform from memory depends upon the situation. Some churches require their pastors to preach without a written text or notes, and you will accept such a call with this in mind. Staged plays, musicals and opera involve memorizing, and only a last-minute substitute may go on stage with a script or score in hand because the show must go on. But unstaged play readings and musical events often do not call for memorization, and in many venues the choice of whether or not to use a score or text will be up to you. Today using a score or text is accepted not as a crutch or an anchor but as a tool that can greatly improve your effectiveness.

It wasn't always that way. Some old-school music teachers and reviewers still criticize a soloist's use of notes as unprofessional. They say that you cannot really make the material your own if you don't free yourself from the paper.

Yet musicians who specialize in chamber music, sonatas or classical art songs use scores to show the equality of the performers. For this reason, legendary German lieder singer Dietrich Fischer-Dieskau, who knew his songs backwards and forwards, always held a notebook with texts when he sang in recital. And today's bands have no rigid rules.

Keyboard musicians traditionally used scores until pianist Franz Liszt changed the game. Liszt was proud of his memory, his long hair, and his aquiline profile. To show off the latter, he turned the grand piano sideways on the stage. And so it remains to this day. Liszt's other legacy, playing without a score, has traumatized the generations of nervous musicians who came after him.

There are a few things to keep in mind, however, if you use a score. If you are a pianist, don't lay the music flat on the closed lid of a grand piano even if you think it looks cool. You don't want to look like a goose stretching your neck to see the page. Use the piano music rack.

Singers should hold scores in a way that does not obscure their faces. Holding the music too high is a favorite trick of shy singers. *Don't hide behind it!* Look up at least once a line; glance toward the last row of the audience. Your eyes must not be glued to the page.

Ministers who preach from memory try to give an appearance of spontaneity, but they usually prepare their remarks beforehand and practice the delivery in front of a mirror. In my opinion as a pastor's wife, denying an eloquent but nervous preacher the use of notes comes close to cruel and unusual punishment. Laypeople should understand that a well-crafted message can also be of the spirit. Cut your preacher a little slack!

Above all, do not feel apologetic about using a memory tool if it helps to control your anxiety. (But in a production involving other performers, check it out ahead of time with the director to avoid misunderstanding.) Teleprompters, cue cards, and ear buds are the norm for those facing a camera in today's world. Why can/t you, too, have the freedom to share your gift without memory panic?

☯

About performance practice.

Since we are on the subject of evolving traditions, let us take a look at the material we perform. Rarely does a concerto or a play fall from heaven perfectly formed. Whatever your venue is—music, dance, theatre, preaching, even karaoke—there are always differing versions. Playwrights rewrite, composers change notes (check out a Beethoven manuscript sometime), choreographers accommodate the skills of their dancers. Why, then, do some professionals insist that the printed score or text (usually a particular edition) is inviolate?

Let me share my theory. The notion of a pure artistic creation arose in nineteenth-century Europe. During a time when the United States was experiencing a religious revival in the Second Great Awakening, the Old World—Europe— became more secularized. Opera composer Richard Wagner epitomized this trend. .In the 1850's he developed a concept of music drama that for many people replaced religious experience as the supreme elevator of the human spirit. Concerts and plays turned into hushed, sacred experiences. Composers like Beethoven, Brahms, Wagner and Tschaikowsky as well as playwrights like Schiller, Goethe, Chekov and Ibsen, wrote works of deep meaning that were performed to silent audiences in ornate concert halls. No programs rustled; no babies cried, no one coughed, nothing was allowed to mar the rapture. They sat with their eyes closed, letting the sonorous sounds bathe their spirits.

This worshipful attitude also applied to the notes on the page and any stage directions. To change the author or composer's intentions in any way was sacrilege. When I was a music student, every note was played or sung exactly as written. If you couldn't handle certain passages, you didn't perform the piece. Singers did not take breaths that broke a phrase (although some teachers let you add in a word here or there if the composer was Handel or Bach). In his memoir *Opera Inside Out,* tenor Robert Mitchell describes how his teacher Marcel Singher insisted he sing long Verdi phrases in one breath in spite of Mitchell's bronchial asthma. Later on Mitchell found a coach who, as he put it, "was more sympathetic to my physical limitations" and helped him rework the troublesome phrases.[45] Straining to meet all the demands of tradition was the norm for musicians of my generation, and we often went on stage in mortal fear of not measuring up.

How times have changed. What was absolute yesterday is no longer so today. I remember how shocked I was when as a teenager I first heard "I'm Always Chasing Rainbows." Such sacrilege—I was naively amazed that a pop musician was "allowed" to steal Chopin's melody! Of course Chopin was long dead and could not defend himself. More "borrowed" classical music followed; "Stranger in Paradise" was swiped from Borodin's "Prince Igor," the Swingle Singers jazzed up Bach, and vocalists of all persuasions began to put their personal stamp on the national anthem.

Devotees of Wagner still make annual pilgrimages to Bayreuth to attend "Ring" performances wearing long gowns and tuxedos, just as their predecessors did a hundred years ago. But even in that hallowed venue, audiences are forced to watch provocative postmodern stagings, like it or not. The era of Nordic divas wearing horned helmets is long gone.

These are bitter times for those who cannot make the transition. One of them is an old friend who years ago renounced a promising career as an operatic bass-baritone. He explained to me why he gave up the stage for recitals and teaching: "I learned my craft from Marjorie Lawrence, a great star," he told me, "and I am not about to desecrate her memory by writhing around the stage in blue jeans."

The ultimate loosening of musical purity happens when a composer invites others to participate in a new creation. According to reporter Sheila Melvin, opera composer Stewart Wallace encouraged his Chinese orchestra percussionists to improvise on their written parts while rehearsing his new opera "The Bonesetter's Daughter" for the San Francisco Opera. "Try it," he urged when a drummer made a suggestion. "The idea for these rehearsals is to let you play more freely, to let you improvise. Let's hear it."[46] Can you imagine a Richard Wagner saying that? Hardly.

The sanctity of the score has been broken through in so many ways that traditional performance practice, or "how the composer intended it," has been demoted to the status of a curious specialty. But the creations of the past are no longer museum pieces. The arts will always be part of the flesh and blood of real people in every sense.

But what do you do if your piano teacher insists that you use certain awkward fingering because it is printed in the score? Chances are that an editor, not the composer, added it. Devise a better fingering and present it to your teacher as an alternative. If a difficult high or low note in a song scares you, can it be changed? If not, can the song be transposed? As mentioned before, transposing has been a practice among famous artists for many years. Today, technology enables the transposition of many scores into any key with the click of a mouse.

◒◓

When time marches on.
Lawrence J. Epstein in his history of Jewish comedians in America describes the anxiety some vaudeville performers felt when the radio broadcasting studio replaced the stage.

Body language no longer counted, and the new medium felt like a strait jacket for visual comedians. Ed Wynn's "mike fright" made his voice sound high-pitched and screechy, so the comedian wore full costume and makeup and performed in front of a live radio audience to counter his nervousness. Many vaudevillians adapted and survived, but not Wynn; performing was never the same for him again.[47]

Traditions whose reasons are long forgotten can take on a life of their own. You may know the one about the mother who always sliced two inches off the end of a ham before baking it. When her daughter asked why, she replied, "I don't know, honey; it's a family tradition. Go ask Grandma." Grandma looked surprised at the child's question. "Why, dear," she answered. "I had to. Otherwise it wouldn't fit into the pan." How often traditions have started like that!

When it comes to dealing with nerves on stage, you no longer must fit into performance pigeonholes that exist for no apparent reason. However, you must be clear about the choices you make and be able to defend them. A good teacher or director will guide you sympathetically with the wisdom of experience. Don't be afraid to ask. After all, they have your best interests and your success at heart!.

CHAPTER EIGHT: YOU'RE ON!

The houselights dim. The audience is quiet. *You're on!*
   Operatic soprano Maria Callas, the greatest singing actress of her time, in later years found this moment so terrifying that she sometimes had to be pushed onto the stage.

You may walk into a brightly lit room clutching notes for your presentation, face a sea of expectant faces, and freeze. You thought the lights would be dimmed.

For many of us, the fiftieth entrance is no easier than the first. Especially when there are surprises—undimmed lights, microphones that don't work, keys that don't play. You vow never to do it again, yet the urge remains. Maybe it will be easier the next time …

The focus of this chapter will be on stage, opera, and recital performance, but much of this information will be equally helpful for anyone who stands in the limelight. You have a message or a talent you want to share, and warbling alone in the woods or preaching to the squirrels isn't enough. In spite of your nerves, you need people in front of you. A poem never recited, a part never played, a sermon never delivered—the longing will not be satisfied until they are shared.

You may not like the irritating nerve bees buzzing around in your head, but you can take the sting out of them. Of course you will be well prepared for your appearance, thoroughly rehearsed and rested and clear of mind. It doesn't matter how unimportant you think a particular event is or how few people may attend. Every time you test the beast's power over your mind. Get ready for even the smallest gig as though you'll give a command performance for the Queen of England!

The following four points are crucial:

1. Check conditions beforehand;
2. Monitor yourself;
3. Visualize your first moments on stage;.
4. Prepare for memory lapses;

Check conditions beforehand.

a. The layout.

Many years ago, violin teacher Carl Flesch described a performer's dilemma that still applies today:

> "Lack of space on the platform, especially when the artist is playing with an orchestra, can indispose an artist for the entire evening. He has agoraphobia in every direction. Too close to the concertmaster's desk, he is afraid of knocking against it. Besides, the first violins are playing all too close to him. If he steps back a little too far, he gets in the way of the conductor's baton, while immediately before his feet there yawns an abyss..."[48]

You may have little influence over the conditions under which you perform. But do find out what they are before you accept an invitation. If you suspect there may be a problem, talk over your concern with the person in charge. You may be able to change something that could cause anxiety. Reasonable adjustments can often be made with advance notice. Two examples.

1. John hated sitting through a banquet meal before he had to perform. He had a nervous stomach; and the smell of creamed chicken and peas was upsetting. He never ate for two hours before singing, yet he was often expected to attend the dinner and sit at the head table. John could make the following suggestion to the organizer: *I don't eat ahead of time, so if you don't mind, I'd like to come a little later and wait in the foyer.* If that was not acceptable, at least he was warned; he could comply, or refuse the engagement.

2. Lynne was asked to appear in a presentation that would be held over the noon hour in a park. She was anxious about standing in the hot sun since she had once fainted in such a situation. When she found out that was to be the case, she made the following suggestion to the director: *I understand that there won't be any shade. May I hold a parasol? I'm allergic to the sun.* (The director agreed and even incorporated the parasol idea into the script.)

A wise New York voice coach once told me to fudge the truth if necessary to save my voice. Sometimes you have to invent an excuse to protect yourself, as professional singers have learned. Insecure conductors and music directors may insist that you sing at full voice throughout rehearsals so they can gauge the orchestra level. Experienced maestros don't need that; they know how to do it using targeted phrases. If you give in, you may not have any voice left for the performance. Plead a cold or a sore throat; hold your ground.

When you question conditions, try to offer an alternative:

— *The podium height doesn't adjust? I'm rather short and I won't be able to see over it; do you have a table?*

— *The soloist always stands perched on those risers? I have vertigo, so I would rather stand on the stage.*

— *The spotlight shines directly into my eyes. Can you direct it a bit sideways? I have a blind spot condition.*

You can't do much about backstage dust, musty smells and irritating cosmetic powders. But be aware of them and take precautions if you have allergies. Sherrill Milnes once described to me how he and his colleagues had to suppress sneezes onstage at the Teatro Colón in Buenos Aires because the venerable old opera house had a revolving stage that stirred up clouds of dust as it creaked its way around to the next scene. It was misery for the singers, but they sang through it.

When I was a teenager in Kansas I played the piano for a musical group that gave programs in grange halls and high school auditoriums. We usually arrived at the last minute, so. I couldn't run a scale on the piano to see if all the keys worked. I found out as I played, and I often had to make snap adjustments in my accompaniments. Since the quality of our programs wasn't a big issue for the local people—they appreciated the fact that we came at all—performing in that venue helped me learn how to improvise while tamping down worries about missing notes.

There are limits to the kinds of special consideration most lay people can expect. Professionals, especially the ones who attract large audiences, get pampering that isn't available to the rest of us. When tenor Luciano Pavarotti recorded for Decca Records, he was allowed to tape his high notes first while he was still fresh. I always envied Italian soprano Renata Tebaldi because she could have her manager check the orchestra's pitch with a tuning fork before every appearance (a pitch of A-440, her preferred level, was written into all her contracts). Pavarotti, on the other hand, considered A-438 "where the juicy sound is."

Opera stars who are in demand routinely transpose arias up or down and provide the orchestral parts. But most singers still have to battle to protect their voices against the upward pressure of conductors and instrumentalists who want to tune to what they consider a more brilliant sound, often A-442 or higher.[49]

In short, don't hesitate to look out for your own interests. There may be more wiggle room than you first imagine.

b. Is there a dress code?

In spite of the anything-goes world we live in, some performance venues still require formal attire. Find out ahead of time if there are any dress expectations. For example, when I was a soloist at Christian Science services, I had to wear a long gown that was color-coordinated with the one worn by the female reader. Many performing groups still have a dress code. Conductor Seiji Ozawa was one of the first to break with tradition when he led the San Francisco Symphony in a black turtleneck sweater and black pants. How courageous he was, we students thought! But he looked very elegant, and soon a lot of performers followed his lead.

Women recitalists used to love the "ooh" reaction from the audience when they swept out in a glamorous satin gown. Today, what you wear on stage will probably be much simpler. But let the color and style of your attire create some good energy for yourself and for the audience. Since you don't want to blend into the scenery, find out about the room decor. Will you be in front of a dark backdrop? Then wear something light-colored. On a light stage, wear a darker color. Be careful on television not to wear reflective fabrics and certain shirt colors.

☙❧

Monitor yourself.

a. Accidents are waiting to happen.

The alarm goes off. Your eyes fly open. The day is here! You jump out of bed and twist your ankle.

Life is full of booby traps. Don't trip on the day you have to perform. *Slow down!*. Just one jerky move, one pulled muscle, and you ruin everything. Get out of bed slowly, one leg at a time. Be aware that when you are excited, every move you make is an accident waiting to happen. Dancers drop a frying pan on a toe, singers burn their throats on coffee, pianists mash a thumb in a dresser drawer; soccer players stumble over toys ...

To avoid any incident, move deliberately and stay focused on your hands and feet. Remember your mother's admonition: *Eyes and hands together!*

Stay in the moment :*the shower floor is slippery ... the cabinet door is open ... the knife is sharp ...*

Pay special attention to sharp objects, pot handles, cabinet doors, strewn toys, family disruptions and distractions. Don't run over your lines while cutting an apple. Don't vocalize while pacing up and down or you're sure to stub your toe on something. Sit down if you talk on the telephone. Outside, watch out for curbs and uneven sidewalks. Remember that metal plates, curb liners and manholes are slippery when wet. Avoid other vehicles on the road.

At the time of Shakespeare, actors and musicians were considered mere technicians without much status. But by the end of the nineteenth century, the most popular performers were idolized by adoring publics and could afford the luxury of no distractions on performance day. Managers, maids and personal valets looked after every need. The morning might begin with a leisurely breakfast in bed, then a bath and perhaps a massage. They might take a walk, warm up their fingers, vocalize, gargle with salt water. They spent the day at rest, unhampered by family responsibilities. After a light early supper, they were driven to the theater.

What a life that must have been! Not much like yours and mine, I'm sure. After working all day we rush home, throw together dinner, give instructions to the family, and run over our lines as we drive to the theater. There is little time to prepare ourselves properly.

Even with such a schedule, try to build in some personal space. You can do a little advance planning. If you have young children, arrange for someone you trust—a spouse, a friend, a family member—to take the kids out for supper on performance night. Spend the time while they are gone preparing yourself. Do breathing exercises. Meditate, close your eyes and visualize a beautiful, calming scene. Take a bubble bath, snooze for half an hour. Hum for a few moments to warm up your voice, practice a few phrases, go over lines.

If your job is hectic, use your lunch hour to provide some mental down time in the middle of the day. When I had operatic rehearsals every evening after work, during lunch hour I often drove to an indoor mall with a courtyard fountain and listened to the soothing sound of the water as I ate my lunch and read something inspirational. This routine kept my "inner beast" at bay and reenergized my core.

Some musicians practice frantically up to the last minute. They hope that focusing their mind exclusively on technique will stave off anxiety. Unfortunately, they find that there is always one more passage to fix until by the time they go on stage they are exhausted and running on nerves. So save your energy for when you are going to need it. Gather strength by resting on the day of performance. It is an important component of your technical preparation.

b. To eat or not to eat?
Eating before performance depends upon how your stomach reacts to stress. Let your gut be your guide! You want to feel energetic but not stuffed, and certainly not nauseous.

If you suffer from anxiety indigestion, don't force yourself to eat a full meal during the day. Take occasional bites of a sandwich if you can get it down, or have some yoghurt. with fruit. Pack a bag with non-sugary granola bars and a thermos of hot tea. Your stomach will unknot eventually. I went through a period when I got the heaves before a performance. While this was unpleasant, it helped to unclench my stomach muscles and the sick feeling then went away. I didn't eat beforehand during that time in my career, and the problem cleared up when I began to practice regular relaxation exercises.

Many athletes fill up on carbohydrates like pasta, potatoes, beans or rice the day before a game to give them a reserve of calories. That can help anyone who shudders at the sight of food on the day of performance. But if you can eat without distress, do it at least two hours ahead of time so it can settle before you go on stage. You don't want a full stomach hindering your breath support, nor do you want to have to burp (or worse) in front of the audience.

When you decide what to eat, have mercy on those who have to stand with you! I sang with a tenor who insisted that to sustain his energy level for a whole evening on the opera stage, he had to down a plate of spaghetti and meatballs beforehand. His garlicky breath tortured at least one queasy colleague—this author—and talking to him about it had no effect. It took a word with the director and some improvised stage business to get through those performances!

If you use your voice, avoid anything that can produce phlegm or cause hoarseness. Milk, sugar, honey, and lemon are problems for many people. Use a process of elimination to see what affects you. (Phlegm can also be brought on by nerves, unfortunately—the beast at work again.) As in our discussion of allergens, you can be affected by prolonged exposure to older electronic equipment such as a computer monitor. Postnasal drip and stuffy sinuses can be treated by various means; tenor Enrico Caruso opened his sinuses with a salt solution, and Luciano Pavarotti sucked on large quantities of menthol lozenges to clear his passages. Sipping hot tea or hot water also helps to clear the throat. Avoid cold liquids, especially if your throat feels dry.

ೞ

At the theater.
In the green room or backstage, try to avoid unnecessary talking. If you are bothered by the nervous habits of fellow performers, follow the guidelines for people with a short fuse: be courteous but monosyllabic, find a dark corner, bury your nose in your score or script.

If you are a pacer, do it unobtrusively so you don't drive your colleagues crazy. Go behind a backdrop curtain where no one except the stage hands will see you.

Above all, avoid the temptation to complain. I can't count the times I have listened to people griping in the green room—about the temperature on the stage (too cold or too hot), the day they had (wretched), a coworker (impossible). Of course it is nerves. But bellyaching can provoke a backlash from others and feelings get hurt. Don't be drawn into this; remember, the play's the thing. Retreat, meditate, pray. Do the following exercise:

Centering Exercise.
— Close your eyes.
—Touch three fingers to your diaphragm.
— Breathe deeply, expanding your lungs completely.
— Let out the air slowly, lips slightly parted;
— Repeat.

Concentrate on your core and the space you are in. Start to feel the momentum building inside that you will take on stage. If you feel your throat tighten, let your jaw go slack and yawn deeply with your mouth closed

Remember, your performance starts in the wings. Gather your energy like an airplane rumbling down the runway—and let it propel you out into the light.

ଔଓ

On stage.
1.The first entrance.
Whether you stride onto a spotlit stage with a dark abyss beyond the footlights, or enter a bright room filled with ex- pectant faces, the first moments are always an adjustment. You feel momentarily off balance, and this is normal. The glar- ing light, the dusty smell of the air, the rustling of the audience may disorient you for a brief moment. Don't be afraid if you "click into autopilot." Your brain will continue work for you.

If you are a soloist, greet your public with a brilliant smile. Acknowledge the applause with a gracious nod or bow (prac- tice this at home). Take your place at the piano, podium or pulpit. Tune your instrument, adjust your sleeves, arrange your papers. Don't blow into the microphone, a common nervous reflex. Remain still for a moment and collect yourself. Think:

I am reality.
I am the present

Nod to the accompanist. Do not analyze. Let it roll.

First entrances are usually less than wonderful. Pianist Joseph Lhevinne, who had to be pushed on stage by his wife, always mangled the first piece on his program.[50] When that was over, he settled down and played brilliantly.

Don't assume that bungling the beginning will be the death of your career. On a Saturday afternoon radio broadcast I heard the Metropolitan Opera debut of a very nervous young soprano. The opera was Mozart's "The Marriage of Figaro." The singer sounded so frightened that she could barely get through her first entrance, the sustained aria "Porgi, amor," Between tortured, breathy notes I heard the voice of the prompter shouting the words. After the aria was over she got control of herself and finished the rest of the opera to loud applause. This inauspicious beginning did not keep Lisa della Casa from a successful career at the Met.

If your opening is shaky and you can't seem to get your bearings, keep going. Make each deep breath count. Your heart will catch up with you and afterwards the audience won't even remember your first entrance.

In former days choreographers, composers and playwrights tried to display the talents of a particular dancer, singer or actor. Today's lyric sopranos who want to sing Mozart must deal with the challenge of "Porgi, amor" whether it suits them or not. For Lisa della Casa, singing at the Met was worth the price of the initial terror. Performing a part that stretches your nerves to that point will require some soul-searching. If you decide to do it, prepare carefully for the extra stress.

If you give a recital, you have the luxury of picking an opening number that shows you to advantage while not taxing your nerves too much. It is most important to give a lot of thought to that first piece. Pianists should avoid opening with a Bach fugue—that is too much pressure for most people. If it has to be from the Baroque or Classical eras, find a "throwaway piece," a number that lets you settle down. If Joseph Lhevinne could do it, so can you. If you are a singer, choose an Italian warhorse like Scarlatti's "Rugiadose, odorose"—it moves along and warms you up and has a repetitive text. Don't open with Handel's beautiful but laborious "Ombra mai piu."

2. Expect memory lapses.
In the previous chapter we discussed whether or not to use a score or text. If you are obliged to perform from memory, you are in the company of nearly all the greats of the past who had no choice in the matter.

Forgetting is a curious thing. Some performers have no problem with memory. They may have trembling knees or a dry mouth, but every note, line, or dance step is right there. Others have to fight for words and notes every minute.

British pianist Myra Hess worried about memory lapses throughout her career. She was especially nervous when she played with an orchestra. She worried because the players would keep going and she had to pick up the thread again somehow. The first time the young performer blanked, she thought to herself: "Well, this is the end of my career." Afterwards as she walked off stage with the conductor, she apologized for the lapse. "Why, heavens," he answered cheerfully, "that was nothing at all. You might have skipped into the second movement, and then we would have had some fun!"[51]

There is a difference between momentary confusion and total blanking. The former clears up quickly and you regain your place. The latter happens when you feel under extreme stress, or are ill or very tired. The brain simply freezes. Do the following three memory exercises as a routine part of your preparation, whether you think it will happen or not:

Memory Exercises.

— Play, sing, speak or dance straight through your memorized material. Do not stop for mistakes unless you get hopelessly stuck. If this happens, find an entry point and try to finish without checking your notes, score or script. Try to unlock your memory by humming a phrase or slowly reciting the alphabet. If nothing works, go back to the beginning and start again without referring to the material. Check it when you are finished with the exercise and practice the weak spots.

— Sitting on a bus or during a break at work, close your eyes and visualize or listen to yourself performing the material from beginning to end.

— In bed with the light off, let the material run through your head like a player-piano roll from beginning to end. If this process makes you nervous, do a breathing exercise as you lie there. When you fall asleep, your brain will be "in the loop."

We heard previously how baritone Robert Merrill forgot the words to the national anthem which he had sung hundreds of times; he simply "la-la-ed" until the rest of the text returned. If this happens to you, resist the urge to race. Make your mind slow down by tapping a slower rhythm with a finger or toe. Focus on words you do remember or use nonsense syllables until your mind clicks in and your memory returns.

If nothing else works and you have to stop, smile at the audience, shake your head, and consult a score or script. In college I accompanied a tenor who blanked at the same spot every time he sang the aria "Una furtiva lagrima." It happened at his lessons and in several student recitals. His teacher ordered him to sing it every week in recital until he could get through it without stopping. It took two months, but he finally succeeded to the great relief and wild applause of the student body.

Audiences are patient. They want you to succeed. Failure is not fatal. Even that most formidable of venues, standup comedy, can be forgiving. The first time Jerry Seinfeld faced an open mike, at New York's Catch a Rising Star, he blanked. He barely managed to blurt out his joke themes: "The beach; driving; shopping; parents!" Then he left the stage and came back to try again another night.[52] So take the pressure off yourself. You are in good company!

CHAPTER NINE: POST MORTEM

In the first chapter we discussed symptoms that strike without warning. After English singer Marianne Lincoln's traumatic first number at her Leipzig debut in 1844, she concluded her diary account as follows:

"Afterwards came the Violin Quartett, & then—'Bel raggio' Well, I was determined to make up for my deficiency, and this went off infinitely better—indeed the applause, the moment I had finished, was tremendous (at least it appeared so to my grateful ears).

But not withstanding all this, I was very much dissatisfied with myself. I have sufficient judgment to know what it ought to have been & also to be aware that I did it much better at Rehearsal. What then is this horrible spell that prevents me from doing justice to my own abilities? Is it to be overcome by reason & determination? If so, shall I overcome it, or shall I remain a slave to this cowardly, childish feeling. ... I write down my feelings thus fully, thinking it may be a useful lesson a few years hence. ..."[53]

You probably understand her feelings. Afterwards you greet well-wishers with a forced smile and say thank-you through gritted teeth, wanting nothing so much as to go home and crawl under the bed. Every flaw races through your brain: *My fourth finger cramped in the Chopin ... The pedal squeak unnerved me ... How could I forget that line ... I couldn't clear the frog in my throat ...*

German dramatist Johann Wolfgang von Goethe spent a lifetime writing and revising a classic play about human dissatisfaction. "Oh, if only I could experience one perfect moment and say, 'stop the clock, it is so wonderful!'" Faust says. In his longing for perfection, Faust trades his soul to the devil for the chance to experience supreme earthly fulfillment.

Behind the glitz and glamour of the stage, there is a different reality. Fans do not see the struggles that accompany success. Athletes, musicians, comedians, actors, dancers, all must deliver in spite of physical and mental exhaustion, aching backs, sore muscles, personal tragedies and depression. Performing is hard work. Only the high moments—and for a few, the financial rewards—make the effort worth it.

But isn't it supposed to be fun? you ask. Well, yes and no. Performing is like raising children. When they are bathed and asleep there is no feeling quite so wonderful as having them. When a performance goes well, nothing can match a deep sense of personal satisfaction.

But is washing diapers, picking up toys, memorizing lines and practicing scales "fun?" Not really. Yes, working can be fun, but it is also often pain and boredom. Your reward comes not from how much fun you have when performing but how the audience receives you. *Your job as a performer is to give it away.*

As a voice student I loved the acoustics of the practice room because the sound I heard in the enclosed cubicle was full and resonant. As my training progressed and I sang in larger halls, I discovered that proper vocal production caused the sound to project outward to the back row of the auditorium. When I was singing correctly, I could not hear myself or the timbre of my voice. I had to learn to trust my technique instead of what I heard in my ears. I had to "give the voice away." This was unnerving, and it took me years to get used to the new reality of "singing by remote control," as a friend put it. The fun of hearing myself would no longer a part of performing experience.

Pianist Van Cliburn once said in a television interview that he did not play for himself. He was performing a service that the members of the audience could not do for themselves. Anyone who shares a talent is doing the same service. To have music, theatre, dance, sports, lectures or sermons, you and I must be willing to give them away.

When you are at home afterwards, record the following information in a diary or on a file:

— the date and place, the program;

— the conditions under which you appeared;

— your emotional state before, during and after;

— what went well and what didn't, and why;

— what made you particularly nervous;

— what you learned that can help you the next time.

Even if at the moment you think there will never be a next time, keep notes. The urge may return. Let the experience resonate in your mind. The Germans have a great word for this process: *abklingen*, to ring down. A church bell rings more gently as it slows down. Let the emotion of your experience resonate quietly in you until it comes to rest. Then put your thoughts to sleep; forget about it for a while. If you can't do that, call up your red balloon and puff your feelings into it.

Finally, always remember that no one does what you do in the same way as you. You are unique. Whether you stand

behind a pulpit or on a stage, whether you face critical colleagues at a meeting or fans on a playing field, remember: you
are surrounded by a cloud of witnesses. They have stood in
the limelight before you, and now they stand with you, behind
you and beside you, urging you on. Feel that presence in your
core as you square your shoulders and go out to face the
limelight. Good luck!

REFERENCE LIST

There is a lot of information available on stage fright. The following annotated list is just a beginning. As you realize what your personal needs are and you are ready to narrow your focus, use this list as a starting point. It can be daunting to face the thousands of entries on the Web. Start your Google or other search with a general phrase—stage fright, performance anxiety, fear of public speaking—and then narrow the results: anxiety drugs, nervous symptoms, Alexander technique, exercises, and so forth. Since web sites come and go, I mention only a few of them here.

Many of the references below have extensive footnotes and bibliographies themselves. Check these for further clues to guide you as you narrow your particular search.

I. Biographies, autobiographies, interviews (listed by performer)
Ankiel, Rick. "A mound of troubles," in *The New York Times Magazine*, Feb. 11, 2001. p. 56. The anxiety of a young left-handed baseball pitcher

Argerich, Martha. "Once-shy pianist tells, um, not quite all," in *The New York Times*, Arts & Leisure, August 3, 2008, p. 19. Interview with reporter Vivien Schweitzer. .

Callas, Maria. *Maria Callas: The woman behind the legend*." New York: Simon and Schuster, 1981.

Casals, Pablo. *Joys and sorrows: Reflections by Pablo Casals*, as told to Albert E. Kahn. Westport: Touchstone, 1974.

—*Conversations with Casals*, by J. Ma. Corredor. Translated from the French by André Mangeot. New York: E. P. Dutton & Co., Inc., 1956.

Christie, Agatha. *Agatha Christie: An autobiography*. New York: Dodd Mead and Co, 1977.

Eisenreich, Jim. "When anxiety comes to bat," in *The New York Times Magazine*, Mar. 8, 1987, p. 72. The struggle of a baseball outfielder with Tourettes Syndrome.

Epstein, Lawrence J. *The haunted smile: The story of Jewish comedians in America*. New York: Public Affairs, 2002. Describes the anxieties of comedians who had to make the transition from vaudeville to radio.

Feinstein, Michael. "O solo you-oh!," in *AARP: The Magazine*, July/Aug. 2004, p. 32. Helpful tips from a popular entertainer.

Fonda, Jane. "An unscripted life starring herself," in Arts & Leisure, *The New York Times*, May 6, 2001, p. 1. An extensive and candid interview with the actress.

Hackett, Buddy. Interview with Joe Rhodes in *TV Guide*, Oct. 23, 1999, p. 43. Discusses the comedian's retreat from live performing after sixty years due to stage fright.

Hess, Myra. *Myra Hess: A portrait*, by Marian C. McKenna. London: Hamish Hamilton, 1976.

Hurt, William. Quoted in "Walter Scott's Personality Parade," in *Parade Magazine*, Sun., Oct. 31, 1999, p. 2. The actor's experience with the Alexander technique.

Jackson, Jesse. "Jackson closes a chapter," James M. Wall in First Impressions, *Christian Century*, June 21-28, 2000, p. 667. The pastor and activist combats test phobia.

Keller, Bill. CSPAN interview with Brian Lamb on Washington Journal, Sept. 1, 2004. The executive editor of *The New York Times* explains personal reasons for his reluctance to appear on television programs.

Levant, Oscar. *The memoirs of an amnesiac*. New York: Samuel French, 1989.

Lincoln, Marianne. *Début at the Gewandhaus and after: A 19th century singer's diary*." ed. by F.M.H. Harper. New Malden: F.M.H. Harper, 1980.

McGrath, Charles. "Teed off: A duffer's lament," in Week in Review, *The New York Times*," Sun, Apr. 14, 2002, p 2. The golfer describes first-tee jitters.

Merrill, Robert. *Between acts*. New York: McGraw-Hill Books, 1976.

Milnes, Sherrill. *American aria: From farm boy to opera star*. New York: Schirmer Books, 1998.

Mitchell, Robert, with David Schechter. *Opera Inside Out*. Xlibris Corporation, 2000. A tenor's memoir of his career in and around New York City. Contains seven opera synopses and singing advice of particular interest to tenors.

Nordica, Lillian. *Lillian Nordica's hints to singers*. New York: E. P. Dutton and Company, 1923.

New York Mets. "Strikeouts and psych-outs," in *The New York Times Magazine*, July 7, 1991, p.10. The team's management hires a full-time psychiatrist.

Oistrakh, David. *David Oistrakh: Conversations with Igor Oistrakh*, by Viktor Yuzefovich. Translated by Nicholas de Pfeiffer. London: Cassell, 1979.

Olivier, Laurence. *Confessions of an actor: An autobiography*, by Laurence Olivier. New York: Simon & Schuster, 1982.

Paderewski, Ignace Jan. *The Paderewski memoirs*, by Ignace Jan Paderewski and Mary Lawton. New York: Charles Scribner's Sons, 1938.

Slichter, Jacob. *So you wanna be a rock & roll star?* New York: Broadway Books, 2004. Semisonic's drummer battles panic attacks throughout his career.

Tebaldi, Renata. *Renata Tebaldi: The woman and the diva*, by Victor Seroff. Manchester: Ayer Co. Publishers, 1961.

Tesh, John. Larry King Live CNN interview quoted in "Walter Scott's Personality Parade," *Parade Magazine*, Sun., June 4, 2000, p.4. How the "new age" musician overcame stage fright using special exercises.

Travis, Randy. "Trippin' through the crossroads," in Music section, *Time*, July 25, 1988. p. 68. An interview with the country music star.

Vienna Symphony. *Stress and music: A study commissioned by the Vienna Symphony.* Coordinated by Maximilian Piperek. Vienna: Wilhelm Braumueller, 1981.

Wangerin, Walter, Jr. "The pacing preacher," in Between Us, *The Lutheran*, June 22, 1988, p.5. A pastor's weekly bout with stage fright.

II. General literature

Auer, Leopold. *Violin playing as I teach it* Mineola: Dover Publications, 1980, p. 22. Advice for string players in chapter 12: "The nerves and violin playing."

Baran, Alex. "The nervous strain of music," in *Music magazine*, Jan./Feb. 1982, p. 22. Reports on a series of lectures in 1982 co-sponsored by the Eastman School of Music and the University of Rochester Medical Center. Deals with orchestra players' performance anxiety from both the musicians' and the scientists' standpoint.

Benedetti, Robert L. *The actor at work.* Third edition. Englewood Cliffs: Prentice-Hall, Inc., 1981. Lesson Three, "Centering, sounding, and aligning" gives centering exercises that can apply to all performers.

Berry, Cicely. *Voice and the actor.* New York: Macmillan Pub. Co., Inc., 1974. Chapter 2, p. 18 "Relaxation and breathing" discusses breathing and vocal tension.

Berry, Mick and Edelstein, Michael. *Stage Fright: 40 stars tell you how they beat America's #1 fear.* Tucson: See Sharp Press, 2009. Berry, a performing musician and Edelstein, a psychologist, interviewed forty successful performers about how they dealt with stage fright.

Colgrass, Michael. "Coping with stage fright," Speaking of Music, in *Music magazine*, Nov./Dec. 1981, p. 38. The percussionist and composer discusses various methods of combating stage fright, including violinist Itzhak Perlman's living-room preparation for his Carnegie Hall debut and flutist Robert Aitken's experiment with hypnosis (a technique reported in *Music magazine*, Oct. 1981).

Crutchfield, Will. "Tailoring arias to suit the vagaries of the voices," in Arts & Leisure, *The New York Times*, Sun., Oct. 17, 1999, p. 37.

Davis, Adelle. *Let's eat right to keep fit.* New York, Signet Book, 1970 [Rev. ed. 1988]. A classic introduction to the effects of nutrition on bodily function. See especially the index listing "Stress."

Desberg, Peter. *No more butterflies: Overcoming stage fright, shyness, interview anxiety and fear of public speaking.* Oakland, CA, New Harbinger Publications, Inc., 1996. One of many general how-to manuals. This publisher specializes in topics related to performance anxiety.

Esposito, Janet E. *In the spotlight, overcome your fear of public speaking and performing.* Bridgewater, CT, In the Spotlight, LLC, 2005. A psychotherapist and workshop leader uses her own experiences to aid her students in combatting their fear.

Flesch, Carl. *The art of violin playing."* Book 2: "Artistic realization and instruction." Second revised edition. New York: Carl Fischer, Inc., 1930. An aid in understanding the idea of the "inner beast." Helpful also for non-violinists.

Forman, Robert, Ph.D. *How to control your allergies.* New York: Larchmont Books, 1983. One of many books on the subject. Dr. Forman gives an account of his personal experience with allergic reactions and describes the wide variety of triggers.

Gabbard, Glen O., M.D. "Stage fright: Symptoms and causes," in *The piano quarterly*, Winter 1980-81, p. 11. describes Joseph Lhevinne's problems and the fantasies that play in our minds before a performance.

Goleman, Daniel. "For stage fright, rehearsal helps," in *The New York Times*, Sun. June 12, 1991, p. C1. Two psychiatrists conduct studies comparing the use of beta blockers with cognitive behavioral therapy.

Goode, Michael I. *Stage fright in music performance and its relationship to the unconscious.* Marina del Rey: Trumpetworks Press, 2003. Discusses the psychological reasons for stage fright and their effect on performer confidence. Uses composite examples derived from classical musicians as well as examples of actual performers who had no stage fright at all.

Greene, Don. *Fight your fear and win: Seven skills for performing your best under pressure.* New York: Broadway Books, 2002. Sports psychologist Greene believes fear is best attacked through action rather than psychotherapy, by flexing the seven fear-conquering muscles of determination, energy, perspective, courage, focus, poise, and resilience. Greene has various anxiety self-help books; for information, check Google or Amazon.com.

Gruner, Walther. "Voice production," in *Tensions in the performance of music: A symposium edited by Carola Grindea,* New York: Alexander Broude Inc., 1978, p. 56. The importance of total body control in bel canto singing.

Hall, Stephen S. The anatomy of fear," in *The New York Times Magazine,* Feb. 28, 1999, p. 42. What scientists have found out about the nature of fear and anxiety through brain studies.

Holland, Bernard. "Singers join in a lament about rising pitch," in Arts and Leisure, *The New York Times,* Jan. 1, 1989, p. 23. A description of the historical variations in "A" pitch over three centuries, especially as it affected singers.

Howard, Leigh. "Actors and opera singers," in *Tensions in the performance of music,* op. cit. [see Gruner], p. 74. Vocal and body exercises for actors and singers. Useful techniques for anyone who uses the voice in public performance.

Johnson, Keith. *The art of trumpet playing.* Ames: The Iowa State University Press, 1981. Discusses stress arising from various areas such as teachers' attitudes, technical accuracy, competition, need for endurance.

Johnson, Patrick with Hope, Jack. "The disease that almost drove me mad," in *Good Housekeeping,* Aug. 1988, p.48. On being a slave to obsession; it can apply to performers who become overly dependent on a ritual.

Newman, William S. *The pianist's problems: A modern approach to efficient practice and musicianly performance.* Fourth edition. New York: Da Capo Press, 1986. Advice for pianists who get jittery fingers and cold hands when performing.

"Onstage, no great shakes," in Medicine, *Time*, July 5, 1982, p. 48. Discusses experiments using propranolol.

Seymour, Lesley Jane. "Fear of almost everything," in *Mademoiselle*, Sept. 1993, pg. 252. A comparison of shyness with social phobia and topophobia (stage fright).

Shapiro, Sanford, M.D. "The fear of appearing foolish: A look at stage fright," in *Noteworthy: Piano news from Kjos*, Winter 1982, p. 3. A psychoanalyst who plays the piano and flute discusses the damage done by overly critical music teachers.

Shurtleff, Michael. *Audition: Everything an actor needs to know to get the part.* New York: Walker and Company, 1978. In a section called "What fear is," the author tells actors how to focus on the elements of a scene rather than whether the auditors like him/her.

"Stage fright," Show #1022, 20/20, ABC News, June 1, 1990. Hosts Hugh Downs and Barbara Walters discuss John Stoessel's report on stage fright, including Stoessel's own anxiety symptoms.

Tindall, Blair. "Better playing through chemistry," in Arts & Leisure, *The New York Times*, Sun. Oct. 17, 2004, p. 1. The debate over pharmaceutically enhanced classical music performance: should drug testing apply to them as well as athletes?

— "Learning to get by on aspirin, coffee and grit," in Arts & Leisure, *The New York Times*, Sun. July 30, 2006, p. 21. Focuses on the physical demands of dancers in performance.

NOTES

Chapter One: The Nature of the Beast

1 Flesch, *The art of violin playing*, p. 113.

2 Lincoln, *Début at the Gewandhaus*, p. 17.

3 Olivier, *Autobiography*, pp. 260, 284.

Chapter Two: Facing Your Fears

4 Wangerin, "The pacing preacher," p. 5.

5 Christie, *Autobiography*, p. 161.

6 McKenna, *Myra Hess*, p. 40

Chapter Three: The Company of the Great.

7 Casals, *Joys and sorrows*, p. 51.

8 Corredor, *Conversations with Casals*, p. 125.

9 Auer, *Violin playing as I teach it*, p. 197.

10 Oistrakh and Jusefovich, *David Oistrakh*, pp. 92-93.

11 Argerich, "Once-shy pianist tells, " p. 19.

12 Stassinopoulos, *Maria Callas*, p. 219.

13 Ibid., p. 230.

14 Merrill, *Between acts*, pp. 221-22.

15 Caruso, *Enrico Caruso*, p. 76.

16 Nordica, *Hints to singers*. p. 109.

17 Seroff, *Renata Tebaldi.* pp. 101-02m

18 Paderewski and Lawton, pp. 114-17.

19 Levant, *Memoirs of an amnesiac.* p. 252.

20 Ibid., p. 289.

21 "An unscripted life," *The New York Times*, p. 1.

22 McGrath, "Teed off," *The New York Times*, p. 2.

23 "Strikeouts and psych-outs," *The New York Times Magazine*, p. 10.

24 *Stress and music.* pp. 5-7.

25 Ibid., p. 7.

26 Ibid., p. 77

Chapter Four: Snares and Setups

27 Quoted in Brand, "Trippin' through the crossroads," p. 69.

28 Klos, "Standin' in the need of prayer," p. 25.

29 Crutchfield, "Tailoring arias," p. 37.

30 Baran, "The nervous strain of music," p. 25.

Chapter Five: Crutches, Anchors, and Auditions

31 Tindall, "Learning to get by on aspirin," p. 21.

32 Ibid.

33 "Drinking and drumming and how it affects you!" *Modern drummer*, p. 33.

34 Colgrass. "Coping with stage fright," p. 38.

35 Tindell, op. cit., p. 21.

36 Ibid.

37 Olivier, op. cit., p. 254.

38 Ibid., pp. 62-64.

39 Merrill, op. cit., p. 221.

40 Flesch, op. cit., p. 110.

41 Johnson and Hope, "The disease that almost drove me mad," p. 48.

42 Shurtleff, *Audition*, pg. 125.

43 Mitchell, *Opera Inside Out*, pg. 124.

44 Ibid., pg. 125.

Chapter Seven: Purist Tradition

45 Mitchell, Robert. *Opera Inside and Out*, pg. 102.

46 Melvin, Sheila. "Multilayered story, multinational opera," *New York Times*, Arts & Leisure, Aug. 31, 2008, p.21.

47 Epstein, *The haunted smile*, p. 67.

Chapter Eight: You're On!

48 Flesch, op. cit., p. 90.

49 Holland, "Singers join in a lament," p. 23.

50 Gabbard. "Stage fright: symptoms and causes," p. 11.

51 McKenna, op. cit., p. 40.

52 Epstein, op. cit., pp. ix-x.

Chapter Nine: Post Mortem

53 Lincoln, op. cit., p. 17.

Made in the USA